2039

W9-AXI-080

1-26 $1.00

Activism; v. Movement/History

# BEYOND
# SEXUAL
# FREEDOM

# BEYOND SEXUAL FREEDOM

*Charles W. Socarides, M.D.*

QUADRANGLE

*The New York Times Book Company*

DESIGNED BY TERE LOPRETE

Library of Congress Cataloging in Publication Data

Socarides, Charles W
   Beyond sexual freedom.

   Bibliography: p.
   Includes index.
   1. Sex customs.  2. Sex—Psychology.  3. Social change.  4. Sexual deviation.  I. Title.
HQ21.S617    1975     301.41'7     74-24291
ISBN 0-8129-0532-6

*This Book
Is
Dedicated to
My Patients*

# ACKNOWLEDGMENTS

*Beyond Sexual Freedom* is a product of hundreds if not thousands of human contacts—with patients, friends, students, teachers, and professional colleagues. Whether in agreement with me or not, they have been a constant stimulus to the production of this volume as they fortified my belief in the absolute necessity for a psychoanalyst's commentary and evaluation of our sexual times.

Two influences were most important in the writing of this work. The first was that of the late Dr. Sandor Rado, Professor of Psychiatry at Columbia University College of Physicians and Surgeons, Director of the Columbia Psychoanalytic Clinic for Training and Research, whose teachings and writings have been for me an unending source of inspiration and discovery ever since I had the good fortune to be accepted as one of his students at the Columbia University Psychoanalytic Clinic in 1949.

The other has been that of my wife, Barbara Bonner Socarides, who has been a keen, active intellectual partner in this work, arguing each point, forcing me to simplify and clarify, editing and integrating the concepts therein. In large measure, it is her book as well as mine, as without her it would never have been welded into a coherent whole.

A special note of thanks is owed to Gladys Levinson for her valuable suggestions during the early stages of the project.

# CONTENTS

# BEYOND
# SEXUAL
# FREEDOM

# INTRODUCTION

This book is about the present time—a period in our history when sexual behavior and customs are undergoing rapidly accelerating and revolutionary changes. We are exposed daily to an unprecedented abundance of information and misinformation about all aspects of sexuality. Group sex, communal living, homosexuality, sex-change surgery, pornography, the changing role of women, open marriage, and a new sexual liberation have become the concerns of all of us.

The rosy picture of a sexual life of bountiful and limitless possibilities is an appealing one. A closer look at the situation however, reveals that the new promise of orgastic paradise is not without its price. As a psychoanalyst, I find these issues to be an everyday concern in the consultation room, for although sex is a physical act, it is a major psychological event in the lives of everyone. The analyst, because of his specialized training in the techniques of psychodynamic investigation, can examine these current phenomena in search of new insights. In this book I propose to make just such a detailed study of current sexual practices, the nature of their powerful appeal, their motivational origins, and what they hold for all of us—beyond the promise of sexual freedom.

Too often the concept of freedom is understood at only its most superficial level—and now more than ever that is true in the area of sexual freedom. All enlightened people would wish for true sexual freedom, both for themselves as individuals and for society as a whole. As human beings we all deserve a sexual bill of rights granting us the inalienable right to sexual expression and satisfaction in accordance with each individual's needs and desires in the context of joy, love, and tenderness and in the absence of authoritarian and intrusive external restraining forces.

The average person, when asked his reaction to such current issues as pornography, homosexuality, group sex, communal living, transsexual surgery, and the more radical changes in family structure, would probably conclude, why not? As long as nobody is hurt, then what harm can be done? Although most of us are aware of rapidly changing sexual codes, the lives of most of us are rarely directly touched by them. Or so we think.

But changes in sexual behavior do not long remain merely interesting, even amusing, news items in the daily newspaper. If their allure is strong enough, if their promise of sexual utopia convincing enough, then the once-radical, even shocking, forms of sexual behavior gain rapid attention and acceptance, finally becoming full-fledged social and sexual institutions.

And all this in the name of "freedom." Elementary philosophy teaches us that there are two basic forms of freedom: the so-called positive freedom, the freedom "to," and negative freedom, the freedom "from." It is not overstating the case to assert that at this stage in our sexual history we have reached the point where we enjoy society's license to engage in many forms of sexual behavior not heretofore sanctioned on such a wide scale. We can all go to movies and buy magazines which depict our wildest sexual fantasies. Having several lovers at one time is no longer thought promiscuous or shameful. The women's liberation movement has begun to bring women not only social and political equality but also the long-overdue right to demand their own sexual identity. Homosexuals have made great strides in gaining their previously denied acceptance in all areas of life. Individuals have the right to live together in couples or in groups without the former prerequisite of marriage. But all of these rights or freedoms are essentially political and social.

The real confusion comes when we regard the entire area of sexual customs and codes as a political/social one. For it is much more than that. And here is where we must exercise freedom's more elusive side and strive for a freedom *from* propagandizing, a freedom *from* easy answers and empty promises, and a freedom *from* being taken in by a widespread sexual egalitarianism in which we are told that any form of sexual behavior is as good as any other.

In this age of the politicization of virtually every area of our lives, we must defend our precious freedom to make judgments, to discern quality, and to strive for what is best for the individual and makes for his real happiness and enrichment.

Many philosophers, sociologists, and journalists have taken up the very subjects in this book. And yet the peculiar gift and duty of the psychoanalyst is to examine man's *inner* strivings and motivations—to offer new paths to self-fulfillment.

For the most part psychoanalysts deal with a current situation and its deep roots in the past. It is undeniable of course that the past continually lends us legitimate clues to the future, not only in an individual's life but in the life of civilization. It is therefore in the belief that man, armed with enlightened self-knowledge, can alter a seemingly disaster-bound course, that I open this book by turning to Robert Anderson's play *Solitaire*.[3] His depiction of our sexual future is a grim one; but one that must serve as a warning to us all, a glimpse beyond sexual freedom.

His central character, the man of the future, is alone. He has no family. He has a number and a lifetime identification card. In this world of the future, reading is not taught, and only the older people, the "leftovers," can read. He "relaxes" by visiting Servocel units where he may stay for twenty-four hours for a certain number of days each month.

A panel of four programs or services is offered, depending on whether he is a man or woman, heterosexual or homosexual. Continuously throughout the period of "relaxation," an opportunity is offered for an "early self-disposal" before the mandatory age of sixty by pressing a button. He is required, if he has a combined Intelligence Quotient–Sperm Qualification Count between 250 and 300, to leave his weekly quota of sperm before the early self-disposal system will operate. If he has an IQSQC of over 300, he is not allowed to avail himself of early self-disposal. Deposit of sperm is mandatory. If he wishes to complain, he may record his "problem" on tape, and a counselor will "handle" his case by tape. There is no human contact.

In the Servocel, he selects "marriage-minus-one" tapes. The titles are "Husband Comes Home," "Christmas Eve," "Bedtime," and "Cocktail Party." He may speak to a tape recording of his wife's voice. If he appears angry or upset, a counselor may interrupt and recommend tapes to diminish frustration, such as "News Ways in Auto-Eroticism." He may obtain a meal by pressing a button, but his menu is pre-selected. He is allowed a one-day work week and is penalized if he is caught working overtime or on any other days. The only thing that is allowed to him that he may elect to do is early self-disposal. "It's the only moment of the day when I really feel alive."

Another prominent member of the cast declares that when the system took over and marriage and family "went by the boards . . . I found people sometimes had a craving for a family or an evening or a special event, so I started 'Call Families.' " However, no sex is allowed during these ersatz family meetings, which are staged by professionals. One is never permitted to see one's own family. But "Call Families" are beginning to become contraband in this new state, and so this too must be carried on secretly. Sam, the hero, cries out in a moment of anguish, "I had a child once, a personal child. One I conceived and brought up, till he was five. It was just during the changeover, when the System was taking over. And when he was five, they came to give him his qualifying examination, and he didn't pass, and they took him away. . . . You know, only so much space, air, food. . . ."

Sam is not allowed to touch or make love to a woman. He is certainly not allowed to live with a family, and his own wife has elected early self-disposal rather than endure this agony. He pleads, "Please, please, I couldn't live without . . . this once a week, and my tapes of my marriage. . . ." As he presses the final button of early self-disposal, he changes his mind. He wants to leave the Servocel, but he is told, "We are sorry. You were warned the last step was irrevocable. Someone else is already breathing your air." He is now a non-person.

The above scene is, of course, science fiction—that is, it is *still* science fiction. But in its depiction of thought control, callous attitude towards human life, and utter despair and helplessness in the individual it may be seen as prophetic. Contemporary man, in pretending to himself that he is not a social organism with social responsibilities, in pretending to himself that he is indestructible, is preparing the way for the end of the human race as we know it. The destruction of the family, the rise in homosexuality, the relaxation of well-founded social legislation such as that against pornography —these are all signs that man has begun to say, "It's too difficult, I give up" in the effort to control those impulses that ultimately militate against his own happiness, both personal and social. But it is also true that man is a creature who has long channeled his energy for his own good and that of mankind—he has created social orders, the smaller one of the family and the larger one of the community. Man has recognized for centuries the need for control, for cooperation, for the attempt to maintain health and stability in himself and his kind. So perhaps he will again turn from the brink of his own self-destruction. What follows is an attempt to evaluate man's present perilous course.

# Chapter 1

# SIGMUND FREUD
# STRIKES BACK

### The Fateful Look Within

Sigmund Freud's first discoveries of the unconscious in 1895 were a "small step for man" that was the beginning of a new era of sexual enlightenment, an era of promise, now deteriorating, alas, into a period of great confusion. Despite the technological miracles of the space age, men have not learned to live with their instincts. Our animosities, our deep disturbances, and our large-scale failure to achieve sexual happiness and control over our aggressions will rocket along with us to new planets unless we begin to examine how far we have come in our search to understand ourselves.

Man has long neglected his inner life in the hopes of finding external solutions to his problems. Lewis Mumford,[116, 117] writer, philosopher, and social critic, writes: "It is not the outermost reaches of space, but the innermost resources of the human soul that . . . demand our most intense exploration and cultivation. . . . The prime task of our age is not to conquer space, but to overcome the institutionalized irrationalities that have sacrificed the values of life to the expansion of power, in all its demoralizing and dehumanizing forms."[118]

Whenever man plunges himself into such darkness, medicine, and especially psychiatry, is likely to suffer the greatest

depreciation by society—a depreciation akin to that sometimes experienced by a physician when he tells a patient that
his illness is serious and the patient is reluctant to believe
the bad news, citing other less serious cases, their miracle
cures and quick recoveries. It is easier to deny the importance of the disease than to face the complexities and difficulties of treatment. Medical psychology is often more than
merely dismissed, however. Gregory Zilboorg has pointed
out that

> medical psychology bears a much more intimate relation-
> ship to cultural changes than does any other branch of
> medicine, and it is also more closely woven together with
> and more directly an outgrowth of the deeply seated human
> instincts. The scientific approach to medical psychology to a
> very great extent depends on and varies with man's attitude
> toward himself and the outside world. This attitude has
> never been fully objective. . . . Even the Greeks' greatest
> philosophers were either hesitant to admit that the soul
> (mind—seat of reason and emotion) might become ill, or
> they definitely denied such a possibility. Man, whether
> primitive or civilized, always feels too anxious about the
> very thing he considers his highest endowment—his mind.
> . . . In his anxiety . . . in times of stress, he inevitably falls
> into an ambiguous and self-contradictory state in which he
> views the world in a manner of mystic humility and his own
> mind in the light of inalienable perfection.[186]

This combined mystification and self-aggrandizement—a
dual response which is entirely understandable given the
horrors and difficulties of the present time and given our
very real feelings of helplessness in facing them—only distorts and worsens an already dreadful situation. One of the
first signs that the problem is critical is a violent upheaval
in sexual roles and customs.

There is a widespread and growing fear that the abroga-
tion or alteration of our sexual morality and customs, with
vast changes in the male and female sexual roles, will bring
about some form of social and personal disaster. This is not

an unwarranted apprehension. Drastic changes in sexual customs are of vital interest to society, and powerful forces are now moving for change in our society, forces which will not be stopped by appeals to tradition or enlightened self-interest.

Threats about what will happen to society, however, do not have much effect either; nobody considers himself to be society's guardian. The average citizen says he doesn't quite know what these social interests are and, after all, aren't personal decisions about sex a private matter? The answer to that question, contrary to popular opinion, is No.

Psychoanalysis reveals that sexual behavior is not an arbitrary set of rules set down by no one knows who for purposes which no one understands. These "rules" are a product of our biological past, a result of man's collective experience in his long evolutionary march, involving biological as well as social evolution. They make possible the cooperative co-existence of human beings with one another. At the individual level, they aim to create a balance between the demands of sexual instinct and the external realities which surround each of us.

Not all cultures survive, the majority have not, and anthropologists tell us that serious flaws in sexual codes have undoubtedly played a significant role in their demise.[81, 82] When masses of people act similarly in changing their mind about previous sexual customs, their collective behavior will, in the last analysis, have a profound impact on the whole of society. This point contradicts the contentions of so-called sex-liberationists who maintain that sexual behavior is merely a question of personal taste. A break with tradition has already happened, and the changes we are now being subjected to will determine the fate of our society.

Our present crisis has been, interestingly enough, coeval with the greatest scientific advances. More than thirty years ago, Philip Wylie indicted us as a generation of vipers, declaring that science, by setting out to increase worldly goods, has "contributed virtually nothing else to mankind. . . . Man's physical senses were extended enormously, [and] the degree and the speed of that achievement are indeed the most common sources of our contemporary vanity. . . . They form the whole preposterous case for the claim that we are civilized. No other attributes of man were in any way either extended or vitalized by science in the last fifty to seventy years. Man's personality, his relations with other men, his private ethics, his social integrity, his standards of value, his love of truth, his dignity or his contentment, were not even potentially improved by the scientists."[185]

Wylie's pungent words stung us but did not sufficiently awaken us to a recognition of our real situation: "A few suits of clothes, some money in the bank, and a new kind of fear constituted the man differences between the average American today [1940s] and the hairy men with clubs who accompanied Attila to the city of Rome." The vindication of this observation came when the behavior of Attila's Huns was duplicated by millions of Nazis and, later, even by some American soldiers in Vietnam. These are Western men, remember. Wylie pointed out that the Axis powers of World War II were composed of men "scientific and Christian like ourselves, each acting from an environment as modern as that of Chillicothe, or my own city of Miami Beach. . . . Each had studied science and each had gone to church—each of the millions—and yet each was able to embrace rape, murder, torture, larceny, mayhem and every other barbarous infamy the minute opportunity spelled itself in letters acceptable to him."[185]

Wylie believed that man could apply the scientific lessons of psychoanalysis for the purposes of self-observation, self-improvement, and teaching, that he could "apply logic and integrity to his subjective personality, just as he has done to the objective world. . . . He would find that laws parallel to physical principles ruled his inner life [and] he would find that truth cannot be escaped within, any more than it can be escaped without. He would learn that when he kids himself or believes a lie, or deceives another man, he commits a crime as real and as destructive as the crime of deliberately running down a person with an automobile. . . . New lines of scientific investigation" are in order before it is too late.

For three-quarters of a century the Freudian message has been "look within." But man is perennially disinclined to accept the implications of the doctrines and discoveries of psychoanalysis: that cruelty, avarice, war, violence, illness can be alleviated or prevented only if man develops techniques of controlling his instinctual drives. And, no wonder. In order to prevent these horrors, they must first be acknowledged—a painful enough task. More painful still is that once acknowledged, they can be overcome by a great effort at controlling impulses which, if not pleasurable, at least offer gratification of some sort. In short, the "reasons" for ignoring the need for control are familiar and habitual, man's old easy, concrete, and immediate satisfactions. But the reasons *for* self-control are more complex, more abstract, require more imagination and foresight to comprehend.

Man's failure in this direction has resulted in the abuse of his technological and creative abilities. Technological advances in themselves are not demoralizing and dehumanizing, but man's greatest challenge and victory lie not in the conquest of space but in the conquest of himself. Technology can solve many problems of the external world. The problems which concern us here have to do rather with the inner life of each of us, that which distinguishes us from the beasts who also inhabit the external world and from whom we have evolved.

### The "Onion Brain"

The advent of technological skills is part of man's evolutionary development. Man has a brain which structurally can be compared to an onion or to a cross-section of an ancient sequoia tree, each ring older than the surrounding one. Man has evolved from the amoeba into the beast of prey, thence to anthropoid apes, and finally to his present form; and each evolutionary stage is still, in a sense, with him and capable of affecting his everyday behavior.

A word of explanation about man's "onion brain." In everyone's brain there are hierarchical levels of integration. We are indebted to Sir Charles Sherrington,[141] J. H. Woodger,[184] W. B. Cannon,[24] and Sandor Rado[126] for their initial conception of neurological and psychological hierarchical levels of functioning, levels which may be compared to the layers of an onion, one on top of the other, each layer capable of being peeled off from the other. These layers are products of one's own phylogenetic and ontogenetic development. A practical demonstration of this structural relationship is found when coma is produced experimentally through increasing insulin dosage. One can observe a human subject "travel" backward in time through the developmental stages of his phylogenetic past, finally reaching the stage where his only response is to painful stimuli applied directly to his body. At that point he can be said to be at the level of the amoeba, the one-celled animal. At this level the only response left is to direct bodily stimuli; it is automatic and thoughtless. Many people operate at this level much of the time, particularly in times of acute stress.

At a higher level than the amoeba, thousands of years later in evolution, we find the level of *brute emotion,* the level at which the beast of prey makes its appearance. Above that is the stage of *emotion-bound thinking,* thought dominated by emotion, a stage introduced by the appearance of the lower primates. This form of thinking aims to mobilize for action and then to act with the rationalization that the emotion justifies the action taken. At the highest level is *intellectual and creative thought;* social affectivity (the emotions of joy, tenderness, gratitude, pride) and technology, science, philosophy, and art made possible by the tremendous growth of man's cerebral cortex. This is the level of man, of homo sapiens. At this point man has the infinite capacity for the productive utilization of all the inherent gifts which evolution has bestowed upon him. It is the *misuse* of these very same capacities and endowments which

leads him to the wanton excesses and destructiveness unknown to the lower species—unknown to them because impossible for them to commit. Under such conditions man can
become more bestial than any beast. Not only does man
justify such actions, he takes *pride* in them. His perversity
allows him to lie to himself, and he becomes a new kind of
beast, *the beast of pride*—of false pride—who nonetheless
thinks, feels, and creates. This creature—who is us—is the
paradox of the present moment. He is a creature of extraordinary endowments, both psychological and physiological.
His powers are great, for good or for ill—so great, in fact,
that it seems as if whatever decision he makes, whatever
direction he takes, must be the final one. All around us we
see evidence that man—this creature of such great power
and capacities—is in the process of making a choice about
the future of the species. And, at the moment at least, this
choice seems marred by a crucial failure.

Man's crucial failure is that he has been unable to manage
the "beast" within himself. He has been unable to collect
and integrate inner knowledge in order to employ it in the
service of emotional fulfillment, the capacity for love, for
understanding the gratification of his instinctual needs in
a way beneficial to himself and to society. When he regresses
to the level of emotional thought, brute emotion, or even
lower and further back in his primitive past to sheer hedonic
responses (of either elemental pain or pleasure), technology
becomes a dangerous toy in the hands of the beast of pride
—dangerous as much because of the way it clouds the issue
of what is really important in life, as because of what technology can do.

## The Summoning of Demons

But why hasn't man learned what is truly important and
how to achieve a better life? And why has he largely ignored
the help of medical psychology? In a paper written between
1915 and 1917, Freud explained man's fateful disinclination

to allow psychoanalysis to help instruct and guide him toward a better life.

By . . . emphasizing the unconscious in mental life, we have called forth all the malevolence in humanity . . . [toward] psychoanalysis. Do not be astonished at this, and do not suppose that this opposition relates to the obvious difficulty of conceiving the unconscious or to relative inaccessibility of the evidence which supports its existence. I believe it has a deeper source.

Humanity has, in the course of time, had to endure from the hands of science two great outrages upon its naïve self-love. The first was when it realized that our earth was not the center of the universe, but only a tiny speck in the world system of magnitude hardly conceivable; this is associated with the name of Copernicus, although Alexandrian doctrines taught something very similar.

The second was when biological research robbed man of his particular privilege of having been specially created, and relegated him to a descent from the animal world, implying an ineradicable animal nature in him: this transvaluation has been accomplished in our time upon the instigation of Charles Darwin, Wallace and their predecessors, and not without the most violent opposition from their contemporaries.

But man's craving for grandiosity is now suffering the third and most bitter blow from present day psychological research, which is endeavoring to prove to the "ego" of each of us that he is not even master in his own house, but, that he must remain content with the veriest scraps of information as to what is going on unconsciously in his own mind. We psychoanalysts were neither the first nor the only ones to propose to mankind that they should look inward; but it appears to be our lot to advocate it most insistently and to support it by empirical evidence which touches every man closely. This is the kernel of the universal revolt against our science, of the total disregard of academic courtesy and dispute, and the liberation of opposition from all the constraints of impartial logic.[49]

Pre-Freudian psychology taught that intellect was supreme and that it was incumbent upon man to control his
impulses by suppressing them. Freud's answer was blunt
and clear; these impulses, he said, could not be suppressed
or they would arise perilously deformed, out of the hidden
recesses of the mind, and give rise to "nervous unrest, disorder and illness. . . ."[187]

Stefan Zweig superbly sums up man's confrontation with
psychoanalysis:

> Free from illusions . . . , relentless and radical, Freud
> showed that the impulsive energy of the libido, though
> condemned by the moralists, was an indestructible part of
> the human organism, a force that could not be annulled so
> long as life and breath remain, and that the best way of
> dealing with it was to lift it into the conscious where its
> activities would be free from danger.
>
> The old method had aimed at covering it up. He aimed
> at its revealment. Where others had cloaked it, he wanted
> to lay it bare; where others had ignored it, he wanted to
> identify it. No one can bridle impulses without perceiving
> them clearly; *no one can master demons unless he summons*
> *them from their lurking places and looks them boldly in the*
> *face.* [Italics added]
>
> Medicine's . . . business is not to maintain silence con-
> cerning the secret places of the heart, but to discover them
> and tell the truth about them. . . . Freud insisted upon
> the urgent need for self-knowledge and self-avowal, for the
> disclosure of the repressed and the unconscious. In this
> way, he began the cure not only of numberless individuals,
> but also of a whole epoch that was morally sick, a cure that
> was to be effected by the removal of its repressed funda-
> mental conflict from the realm of hypocrisy to the realm of
> science.[187]

Concurrent with Freud's discovery of free association,
which enabled man to view the hidden aspects of his psychic
life, another physician, Karl Roentgen, discovered the X-ray,
which allowed man to examine the hidden recesses of his

body. This confluence of events seemingly left no barrier to man's scientific study of himself. Yet technology has failed to help us master our demons, and that failure is as much a result of man's fears about those demons as it is a result of the limits of technology. A machine, after all, cannot examine the mind.

Only man can do that. And all he needs to do it is the courage to face the demons. But man also fears his greatest possession, his mind, this repository of his drives, weaknesses, anxieties, guilts, wishes, aspirations, and creative resources. He rationalizes his behavior, makes excuses for the past, and dares not look within because of the very pain this investigation can provoke, denying to himself the relief and healing which is the inevitable outcome of investigating the cause of pain.

Freud taught us about the processes of the unconscious, giving man the opportunity to know himself better; but he could not make man happier just by contributing knowledge. This desideratum requires man's individual perceptive synthesis and implementation. But this synthesis, on a large scale, is missing in our society today.

## The Age of the Polymorphous Perverse

While no one now alive has remained totally untouched by Freudian concepts as they permeated the various disciplines—pedagogy, art, science, history, medicine, literature, sociology, theology—the integration of these concepts into our world community has been vastly inadequate, and the concepts are now under wholesale attack and threatened with extinction. The reason for this attack is the general resistance to facing a central human and social problem: how best to reconcile the interests of society with those of the individual in a day and age which places the highest value on what constitutes a false concept of individuality.

The essence of the present issue was noted by Freud in

*Civilization and Its Discontents:* "Liberty of the individual
is no *gift* of civilization. . . . The development of civilization imposes restrictions on it, and justice demands that no
one shall escape these restrictions. . . . A good part of the
struggles of mankind center around the task of finding *an
expedient accommodation—one, that is, that will bring happiness—between this claim of the individual and the cultural
claims of the group;* and one of the problems that touches
the fate of humanity is whether such an accommodation can
be reached by means of some particular form of civilization
or whether this conflict is irreconcilable."[17] [Italics added]

Freud's therapeutic principle, the uncovering of the unconscious so that man could integrate his sexual and aggressive drives into his ego, implied a hope for self-improvement
in the most humanistic sense—an improvement which includes control of impulses, both sexual and aggressive, and
the addition of those dynamic forces to the ego which strive
for higher aims and against self-deception or hypocrisy. In
Freud's own words, "the work of psychoanalysis puts itself
at the orders of precisely the highest and most valuable
cultural trends, as a better substitute for unsuccessful repression." Freud believed in the *moral* effect of psychoanalytic therapy and in the Socratic ideal that the recognition
of truth would inevitably lead to good. Thus, psychoanalysis and psychoanalytic therapy could only make a
contribution to the improvement of man and the melioration
of his condition. Freud's hope, of course, was that man
wished to know the truth, whatever it might be, and that
he would follow where it led. Some of these truths, however,
would prove difficult for men, as individuals, to come to
terms with.

Our social and cultural institutions, which go far to create
man's condition, derive, to a considerable extent, from the
successful sublimation of our sexual and aggressive instincts.
The trouble lies in the overrepression and overinhibition of
these instincts. Freud warned that if sexual and aggressive
instincts were not mastered, individuals one day might rise

up against their social, intellectual, and creative institutions and destroy them—that the claim of the individual might prove to be stronger than the claim of the group.

Psychoanalysis frees man from the rationalizations and self-damaging illusions which allow him to put his individual needs above everything else. This freedom, with its concomitant responsibilities to society and its requirement of disciplined self-awareness, is therefore often found to be unbearably difficult to attain. Man's wish to avoid anxiety leads him to seek instant satisfactions, instant solutions, instant pleasures. The contemporary and vitally important factor of transience (so well described by Alvin Toffler in his book *Future Shock*[175]) plays an additional and devastating part in abetting modern man's turning away from the study of his inner self.

And so we come to our present era of sexual freedom when anything goes—at least anything sexual, anything aggressive. It is a social era which bears a strong resemblance to the stage of individual human life found in early childhood. Every child traverses a developmental period in his earliest years in which all sexual objects and aims are entertained and engaged in, instinctively and without restraint. This is a time of confused but emerging sexual-role identity, part of normal development, a period referred to as the phase of *polymorphous perverse sexuality.*[42]

There are striking similarities between this infantile period and the revolutionary trends of today. The present Age of the Polymorphous Perverse is characterized by group sex, advocacy of sexual perversion, obscenity and pornography, unrestrained sexual license, the proliferation of gender-role confusion, and the eradication of sexual-role differences between men and women.

Those caught up in the pseudoliberation of the Polymorphous Perverse behave astonishingly like the victims of another sexual era—that of the pre-Freudian sexual suppression. Both groups are characterized by denial: neither channels nor properly uses the sexual instinct. This is negation of sex which in our time takes a most curious form—it wears the mask of the wholesale release of all sexual expression (in direct contrast to the former suppression). But the end result is the same: lack of appreciation and understanding of the sexual instinct in its *healthy* manifestations. Psychoanalysis, on the other hand, rather than taking a position of either rigid suppression *or* wild abandon with regard to sexual questions, seeks to discover what is good for the human organism and what is bad for it, what makes for growth and enrichment of the personality and self, and what makes for its destruction and impoverishment. In short, it says that sex should make the world a better place for men and women, as individuals *and* as a society.

# Chapter 2

# MALE OR FEMALE

The human condition, by its very nature, is full of distinctions, differences, relationships, and choices. Man's fate, first of all, is to be born either male or female. The advent of *sexual* reproduction (which yields endless combinations of characteristics from the joining of two dissimilar cells) as differentiated from reproduction through *asexual* fission (in which an organism reproduces simply by splitting into two *similar* cells, no partner required) was a significant development in evolution. We are continually forgetting this fact of life, so basic to our very existence. But the point of this seemingly academic observation is that the emergence of sexual reproduction was possible only through the cooperative union of two different cells, male and female, and later in the course of evolution, of two distinctly different individuals. The fact of reproduction thus creates a bond between the sexes.

This vital bond becomes man's nemesis—when the differentiated roles of the two sexes break down. Freud believed that this breakdown was the major problem of mankind:[48] men and women fail to come to terms with qualities of the opposite sex, both those which reside in their partner and those which reside within themselves. People thus cannot be happy with themselves or with each other until they come to terms with their "bisexuality." This does not mean that men and women, alongside a supposedly innate sexual desire for a person of the opposite sex, harbor a comparable desire for a person of the same sex, as this term is popularly misconstrued. Rather, Freud believed that we should loosen the connection between sexual instinct and sexual object-choice, a choice which in any case is learned behavior, beginning in childhood and dependent upon an earlier-established sense of sexual or gender identity.[42]

There are immutable contrasts and complementarity between the sexes. The *contrasts* are measurable and inspectable and verifiable at a purely physical level; in addition to the primary genital differences there are other anatomical differences, the secondary sex characteristics: skeletal system, skin texture, size of vocal cords, fat distribution, etc. The *complementariness* can be conceptualized as the *push-pull principle*. Male sperm cells seek the egg as the egg attracts the sperm. Male penetration acts as a pressure pump just as the female response acts as a suction pump. At the level of the total individual, the male seeks out, arouses, and penetrates the female. The female, according to the principle of pull, either by "passive" presentation or by active cooperation, attracts and embraces the male.

An understanding of the push-pull principle (like those of gravity, speed of light, conservation of energy, upon which we base our understanding of the physical world) can do much to explain the basic emotional differences between men and women.

Much sexual confusion has surfaced recently, in attempts to find the source for sexually differentiated behavior, because it is extremely difficult to tell which aspects of female or male behavior are part of organic equipment—that is, of organic evolution—and which are part of social evolution or a result of social conditioning. In an era in which sexual roles are being reexamined and defined, confused and even destroyed, it is vital to identify these aspects.

The eminent psychoanalyst Sandor Rado introduced the push-pull principle but stopped short of its complete psychological elaboration as regards adaptation between the sexes.[124] The evolutionary adaptation of push-pull (suction pump and pressure pump) was apparently in the interest of fitness for survival. It mandates complementary action between the sexes and its unparalleled adaptational value is unique. Because the concept makes clear that both men and women are active in any interchange between them, it effectively negates the long-held proposition of uniquely male "activity" and uniquely female "passivity." It can help bring men and women together in love, confidence, cooperation, and shared interests, transcending egoistic impulses. It is the foundation for the mechanism of falling in love—but at the same time it can be the source of great misunderstanding between men and women.

Even when men and women experience the sexual act together, it may have different meanings for each. This difference reflects itself not only in the sexual sphere of behavior. Men and women also interpret nonsexual activities differently; they occupy a different place in the lives of each. Yet complementarity is a powerful force increasing our ability to survive, promoting productivity, mutuality, and cooperation.

The necessity for a man to be a man and secure with this fact, and for a woman to be secure in her womanhood, is crucial. This necessity—on which individual relationships (and indeed society itself) are based—is now in jeopardy. The recent enthusiasm for so-called sexual freedom has called into question sexual identity itself, the very identity which defines us and enables us to expand and function in complex and varied spheres beyond the sexual.

The gradual eroding of the basic concept of male *or* female, under the guise of sexual freedom, has led to the acceptance of unisex and of homosexuality as a valid and normal form of sexual life, to the emergence of change-of-sex surgery to "alleviate" sexual pathology of purely psychic origin, to an undermining and destruction of the importance of the intimate and affectionate components of the male-female sexual pair as seen in group sex, to the nation's inundation by obscenity and pornography, and to the threatened destruction of the family.

# Chapter 3

# WOMEN'S LIBERATION

In recent years the women's liberation movement has brought about a reinterpretation and restructuring of the role of women in virtually every aspect of daily life. What began as a revolution against social and economic bondage has taken on the dimensions of a movement which goes to the very core of our society. Women are going into professions previously restricted to men. They are seeking equal representation in government. The housewife who, ten years ago, was content—or at least felt she should be content—to stay at home in a purely domestic role is now finding the time and responding to the inclination to be a more vocal and active member of her community.

Hand in hand with the social and economic manifestations of the new liberation is a movement which demands of the individual woman that she seriously examine and redefine her sexual role. It is in this area that the greatest confusion exists for both men and women. It is also in this area that women have the most to lose.

The current feminism can be divided into two major categories: one, the reform movement; and two, the more radical women's liberation groups. The first is exemplified by NOW (National Organization for Women), which is an activist civil-rights organization using traditional democratic methods for winning legal and economic rights, attacking mass-media stereotypes, and featuring the slogan "Equal rights and partnership with men." Reform feminists, according to Gerda Lerner, "cooperate with the more radical groups in coalition activities, accept the radicals' rhetoric, and adopt some of their confrontation tactics; yet essentially they are an updated version of the old feminist movement, appealing to a similar constituency of professional women."[96]

The second category consists of small proliferating independent women's liberation groups, significant far beyond their size. These groups, according to Lerner, support most of the reform feminist goals "with vigor and at times unorthodox means; but they are essentially dedicated to radical changes in all institutions of society. They use guerrilla theater, publicity stunts, and confrontation tactics, as well as standard political techniques. Within these groups there is a strong emphasis on the re-education and *psychological reorientation* of the members, and an interest in fostering a supportive spirit of 'sisterhood.' "[96] [Italics added]

While all feminists share a justified indignation at their second-class citizenship and economic handicaps, Lerner continues, there is a "determination to bring . . . legal and value systems into line with current sexual mores, an awareness of the psychological damage to women of their subordinate position, and a conviction that changes must embrace not only laws and institutions, but also the minds, emotions, and sexual habits of men and women."

Certainly all enlightened people agree with feminists in their aim to unburden themselves of second-class citizenship and the suffering imposed by discrimination, indignities, and economic exploitation. Some feminist demands are entirely reasonable; some, however, are not. Radical feminists demand changes in the content of school and college curricula in the areas of psychology, sociology, and history. Wholesale revisions (and in some cases, reversals) in social and domestic life seem to them to be necessary either as reforms, as reparations to a victimized sex, or as part of a large-scale rejection of a former identity. They want, according to Lerner, an end to the patriarchal family, "new sexual standards, a re-evaluation of male and female sex roles. Their views regarding sex and the family are a direct outgrowth of the life experiences and life styles of the younger or 'pill' generation, the first generation of women who have control over their reproductive functions, independent of and without need for cooperation from the male. This has led them to examine with detachment the sexual roles women play."[96] Furthermore, female frigidity is regarded by many of them as a male-invented myth.

The most important radical feminist goal is

> their rejection of the traditional American family [which is] challenging our institutions most profoundly. . . . They consider the patriarchal family, even in its fairly democratic American form, oppressive of women because it institutionalizes their economic dependence on men in exchange for sexual and housekeeping services. They challenge the concept that children are best raised in small nuclear families that demand the full- or part-time services of the mother as housekeeper, cook and drudge. They point to the kibbutzim of Israel, the institutional child care facilities of socialized countries, and the extended families of other cultures as superior alternatives. Some are experimenting with heterosexual communal living; communes of women and children only; "extended families" made up of like-minded couples and their children, and various other innovations. They face with equanimity the prospect of many women deliberately choosing to live without marriage or motherhood. . . .
>
> Some feminists practice voluntary celibacy or homosexuality; many insist that homosexuality should be available to men and women as a realistic choice. . . . There may be those with strong binding ties to one man, and many are exploring, together with newly formed male discussion groups, the possibilities of a new androgynous way of life. But all challenge the definitions of masculinity and femininity in American culture.[96]

This challenge often takes the form of illogical and sometimes bizarre assumptions and frequently rests on a bewildering confusion of psychosexual issues.

## The Radical Manifesto

One highly articulate leader of the more radical wing of the movement is Germaine Greer, author of *The Female Eunuch,* which attracted international attention. Greer feels there is only one way to improve women's lot: total political revolution in order to produce a completely different economic structure. "No liberation spokesman should lose sight of the fact that her emancipation, her liberation, is an impossibility in terms of the society. This society must be destroyed before her flower can bloom, and her flower is one of the things that are going to destroy this society."[60]

Cambridge-trained Greer has undoubtedly learned from the study of evolution, animal behavior, psychology, and psychoanalysis that beyond the chimpanzee in the evolutionary developmental scale toward man, the only innate (reflex) neural mechanisms in the sexual act that remain in man are erection, or corresponding arousal of genital structures in the female, pelvic thrust, and orgasm. Below the level of the chimpanzee in evolution, all sexual behavior is automatic—the presentation of a certain stimulus will reflexly cause arousal. Above the chimpanzee, sexual activities are almost exclusively motivated by cerebral functioning. So far Greer is correct in her assumption.

She also, however, sees women as struggling to reconcile their education along masculine lines with a feminine condition until puberty "resolves the ambiguity and anchors her safely in the feminine position." When this "anchor" doesn't work, psychoanalysis, according to Greer, is a supporting, intimidating, and coercive technique used against the female at puberty and from thence onward. She feels that the "castration of women has been carried out in terms of masculine-feminine polarity, in which men have commandeered all the energy and streamlined it into an aggressive conquistatorial power, reducing all heterosexual contact to a sadomasochistic pattern." The nuclear family, according to Greer, is no longer a viable institution. She contends that the female has found a new arsenal for the fight against the male in the work of Masters and Johnson, and that woman "must know her enemies, the doctors, the psychiatrists, social workers, marriage counselors, priests . . . and popular moralists."

Greer's major objection to psychoanalysis seems to be that woman is viewed by male psychoanalysts simply as a "sexual object" for the use and appreciation of men. Her sexuality is thus both denied, and misrepresented by being identified as passivity. The vagina is obliterated from the imagery of femininity in the same way that the stigma of independence and "vigor in the rest of her body are suppressed." This objection is based on an assumption which is patently false. Greer's understanding of psychoanalysis seems so perverse as to be obvious distortion. She makes a clear distinction between "feminine" and "feminist" positions, but that distinction is arbitrary and deceptive. To be "feminine" according to psychoanalytic theory is to be among other things independent and self-aware. Only a self-actualized woman is truly feminine. A feminist, on the other hand, seems to be a woman defined purely by ideology, certainly an *external* form of self-definition.

## The Liberated Orgasm

As part of her complaint, Greer boldly asserts that Freud suffered from "anatomical ignorance," as he demanded from women an unattainable goal—that is, vaginal orgasm—as a sign of mental health. Her dethronement of the vagina was followed by an apparent coronation of the clitoris.

The "liberated" orgasm is by no means a revolutionary concept. It has long been known that clitoral stimulation can lead to sexual arousal and orgasm. It is also a clinically proven fact, however, that some women become vaginally anesthetic; they experience absolutely no sensation in the vagina upon its penetration by the penis because fear of penetration provokes anesthesia at the moment of entry. The proof that this fear exists (aside from analytic material gathered in treatment, such as dreams about terror of penetration) is precisely that the clitoris is spared; there is clitoral response *simultaneous* with vaginal anesthesia. When this occurs in a woman who consciously desires to be penetrated, it usually reflects an emotional incapacity to accept phallic penetration and is symptomatic of an *unconscious* fear. As such, vaginal anesthesia reflects difficulties in accepting her psychosexual role in the male-female relationship. It is tied up with certain unconscious fears of damage, whether to the genital itself or to her sense of personal integrity, social functioning, and self-esteem in general. It is essential for the woman herself, aside from any considerations she may have about pleasing her mate, to overcome this fear of vaginal penetration whether or not she can achieve orgasm by other methods, in order to be as fully female as possible.

There is a popular notion that Masters and Johnson have "liberated" the female orgasm from the "straightjacket" of psychoanalysis with their announcement that the dichotomy of vaginal and clitoral orgasms (supposedly fostered by psychiatrists for the psychic enslavement of women) was entirely false. Anatomically, the "new" description states, orgasms are centered in the clitoris, whether they result from the direct manual pressure applied to it or from the indirect pressure resulting from the thrusting of the penis during intercourse and pulling on the structures connecting the clitoris with the vaginal entrance. Female-liberationists greeted this announcement from Masters and Johnson with cries of triumph and elation.

The knowledge that orgasm can be initiated from the stimulation of the clitoris or from other bodily parts—the lips, the mouth, the mucous membrane of the anus, other membrane surfaces, or even the mind alone—is widespread and of long standing. The basic structures which actually partake of the peristaltic contractions in the pelvis are those of smooth muscle, blood vessels, vascular systems, and nervous cells of both male and female pelvic-region organs. Excitation may then spread to adjacent structures. Orgasm, if powerful enough, may in some instances involve the entire skeletal musculature. All these facts were well known to psychoanalysts long before Masters, Johnson, or women's liberation. They do not fundamentally change any aspect of female sexual response.

Additional "new" information was that women are naturally multi-orgastic. Since a woman does not have a refractory period in the structures partaking in orgasm, she is likely to experience or be capable of several orgasms in rapid succession, or as long as there is ongoing "effective sexual stimulation," in the words of Masters and Johnson.[74] Psychoanalysis had been "dead wrong," according to this source, in maintaining that vaginal orgasm is the *sine qua non* of good sexual health in women; orgasms may vary in intensity, these doctors stated, but not in kind. And so began the "do-it-yourself" theory of women's sexual liberation—an aspect of their theory not expected by Masters and Johnson, but one which was nonetheless an outgrowth of it.

Much *physiological* documentation in *Human Sexual Response* was new, but the conclusions about the female orgasm were already known to psychoanalysts. Therefore, the following remarks are not meant to dismiss Masters and Johnson's work, for their observations on *physiological* events accompanying sexual arousal and orgasm are valuable and worthwhile. The psychoanalyst dealing with the intimate *psychic* events of a patient's life and the transference relationship (doctor-patient relationship) could not, needless to say, at the same time engage in sexual physiological studies on the same subject. Furthermore, the frequent derogatory label of "pan-sexualism" attributed to psychoanalysis may have deterred psychoanalysts from researching the physiological events accompanying orgasm. Some studies, however, were made.

I was a student at the Columbia University Psychoanalytic Clinic for Training and Research from 1949 to 1952, and the same information on female orgasm was then common knowledge and an important part of our instruction there. The professor of psychoanalysis at that time was the late Dr. Sandor Rado, formerly head of the Educational Division of the New York Psychoanalytic Institute, and before that Director of the Berlin Psychoanalytic Institute. For many years he had been responsible for much of the curriculum at psychoanalytic institutes in this country. Rado's views were clearly expressed in an article published in 1949, nearly twenty years before publication of Masters and Johnson's "new" findings:

> Orgasm in the male is attendant upon the production and delivery of sperm; in the female upon the receiving of sperm. This fact of reproductive anatomy helps to explain the clinical observation that *the orgastic requirement of the sexually strong healthy female by far exceeds that of the sexually strong healthy male. Orgastic requirement is measured here in terms of desire, a capacity for frequency, in particular for serial or multiple orgasm.* . . .
>
> Orgasm . . . is the final goal in this coital pleasure pursuit. Moreover, the orgastic pleasure scheme is considerably enlarged through contributions derived from extragenital sources. Therefore, it is apparent that orgasm may be elicited from any number of sources, the clitoris, the vagina, the tip of the nose, the earlobe, the lips, or any other pleasurable point of origin. However, it is the same structures which go into orgastic peristalsis. . . .[124]

But whether Masters and Johnson or Rado explains the condition of orgasm, men and women should realize that the conditions for sexual happiness do not lie in such isolated items as orgastic potency alone and apart from the emotional relation to one's mate; that there is no such thing as absolute sexual compatibility. They must learn to be more tolerant of the partner's difficulties and this, in turn, will have the effect of lowering the exaggerated expectations they have of themselves. After all, sexual pleasure rests on far more than sexual technology.

## *Lesbianism*

Heterosexuality is not alone in Greer's reevaluation of sexual practices. Her views on lesbianism are representative of the widespread misconceptions of the radical wing of women's liberation:

> Much lesbianism, especially of the transvestite kind, may be understood as a revolt against the limitations of the female role of passivity, hypocrisy and indirect action, as well as rejection of the brutality and mechanicalness of male sexual passion. All forms of lesbianism involve an invention of an alternative way of life, even if the male-female polarity survives in the relationship to the degree that there is butch and bitch within it. The prevalence of tribadism as a principle lesbian mode of lovemaking argues the relative unimportance of the masculine fantasy in the relationship. However, sexual deviations have been treated with so much lecherous curiosity and violent insult that most lesbians are unable to make of their choice an alternative anything like a political gesture. The operations of relentlessly induced guilt and shame cause the lesbian to conceal her condition, and to mis-state her own situation as the result of a congenital blight or the mistakes of her parents. It is true that her inability to play the accepted role in society probably results from a failure in conditioning, but that is not itself a disqualification from the ability to *choose* lesbianism in an honorable, clear-eyed fashion, rejecting shame and inferiority feelings as a matter of principle, whether such feelings exist or not. The lesbian might as well claim that she had no other acceptable course to follow and become the apologist of her own way of life. Unfortunately, too often she is as blinded by spurious notions of normality as her critics are.[60] [Italics added]

This lengthy statement is replete with rationalizations, false assertions of "fact," and ignorance of the psychodynamics of female homosexuality. First of all, the lesbian *has* no choice in her sexual predilections and because of this she must be helped, understood, and accepted. It is a serious error to say that any women "choose lesbianism." In the true obligatory homosexual the condition is unconsciously determined, as differentiated from the behavior of a person who deliberately engages in female-female sexual contact due to situational factors or for variational "kicks." It is furthermore inaccurate to state that lesbianism is really a revolt "against the limitations of the female role," against its passivity and hypocrisy. The nuclear core of homosexuality is never a conscious choice, an act of will. Rather it is determined from the earliest period of childhood (in terms of its origins, of course, not its practice). By age three a child who will become a homosexual in adolescence or adulthood can be clinically identified by obvious tendencies. The girl is unable to accept her identification with her mother as it involves identifying with a cruel and destructive figure who, she believes, will not allow her to achieve autonomy and independence as a human being. However, to break from this hated mother means the loss of love, for the child is convinced her father also does not care for her, simply because she is female. Observations presented by unqualified sources as if they were valid clinical data misinform the general reader and mislead the unfortunately vulnerable public.

## Psychoanalysis and Liberation

Greer calls psychiatry "an extraordinary confidence trick" and deplores the fact that psychology persuades men and women to seek the cause of emotional difficulties within themselves. The idea, expressed in *Female Eunuch,* that psychoanalysis "brainwashes" patients into accepting concepts, ideals, and "enforced happiness" because of the *Weltanschauung* of the analyst is folly and nonsense. Basic to psychoanalytic therapy is the rule that the doctor should not attempt to remake the patient in his own image. The doctor is ever watchful that the patient, in the course of bettering his own life and actualizing his potentialities, not simply adopt the analyst's beliefs as his own and thereby repeat a false security technique begun with his parents. Such a technique would be invariably doomed to failure, as it does not arise from inner resolution of conflict. Every analyst knows the patient's happiness belongs to himself alone.

Likewise, women patients are not treated as Greer asserts; they are certainly not made to conform or induced to accept, in her term, "female servitude." In actuality, the therapist works to develop to the fullest the innate capacities, abilities, and self-reliance of patients. If the patient is capable only of self-defeating "happiness," its dynamic basis is laid bare and the patient has a choice for the first time in her life—a choice previously unavailable to her conscious mind. This discovery and opportunity are the real value of psychoanalysis and therein lies its function: to afford a person a choice of response to present-day events which are anachronistically distorted, influenced as they are by the faulty responses developed in early childhood.

Freud and his followers do not speak of intrapsychic conditions of castration anxiety, penis envy in the female, clitoral versus vaginal sensitivity, and orgasm in terms of a value system, as some women's-liberationists claim. They simply *observed* scientifically the workings of the mind and the underlying pathological conditions which existed there: the fears, anxieties, and guilts of an unconscious nature which should not be there. However, like the eight unearthed cities of Troy, layered scenes of old and tragic wars, these unhappy conditions (castration anxiety, penis envy, fear of engulfment by the vagina) were found through mental excavation to exist and to exert a damaging effect on the individual's current functioning. They cannot simply be wished away, nor can the damage they have done be wished away.

The existence of these phenomena of mental life has been misconstrued by some radical members of the feminist move-

ment to indicate that Freud maligned women. Such an attitude is a self-imposed loss, for Freud felt that by the very
elucidation of these pathological facets of human development, female sexuality as well as male sexuality would, subject to conscious alterations, become more rewarding, fulfilling, and gratifying.

## Female Chauvinism

We cannot leave this chapter without presenting a rational and enlightened view of the women's-liberation movement. It emanates from one of its founders, Betty Friedan,
who believes the rights of lesbians are not an issue.

> Sexual politics makes man the enemy and ignores the
> sexual reality, the relations between a man and a woman.
> Lesbians, for whatever reason, have repudiated two as-
> pects—sexual feelings for men and child-bearing. They
> would alienate the women who can't identify with the rhet-
> oric of sex class warfare and alienate men unnecessarily,
> if their thinking were allowed to take over the movement.
> If they are homosexuals first, then they are a danger to
> the movement and will pervert the priorities. We shouldn't
> bar anyone from the movement but we shouldn't let the
> movement be disrupted either.
> I warn against female chauvinism and against the danger
> of taking an abstract ideology, based on obsolete theories
> of class war or separatist racial theories, and applying it to
> the situation of women. . . . The question is, will the
> women's movement be a two-sex movement of human rev-
> olution or will it be perverted by female chauvinists into
> sex class warfare?[50]

Enmity between men and women solves nothing—the cause
of our miseries lies, as always, not at the feet of another but
within ourselves—men and women alike, men and women
together.

## *Meierhofer's Babies and the Loss of Motherhood*

Sex warfare is not the only disastrous outcome of radical feminism. Fifty years ago, even the most ardent feminist would not have asked that the family be abolished. The most that any feminist of that era would have dared to demand would be that children over two be kept in nursery centers for two or three hours daily. Now feminists declare that the family unit as such need not be preserved. They believe both parents can work and that children should be taken care of in state-subsidized facilities.

Most psychiatrists know that leaving children in day-care centers for prolonged periods, especially during early infancy, can have a deleterious effect. This is an unpopular view in this era of deemphasizing individuality, but it is well founded. Clearly the day-care centers cannot be a substitute for the home. If entered too early, for example at the age of two, the effects are likely to be worse than at the age of four. Children at the earlier age have too difficult a time in competition with their peers, and emotional rapport with adults is tenuous.

Swiss child psychiatrist Dr. Marie Meierhofer explains that depression is common even in infants no more than three months of age, especially in those who have been placed in nurseries by working mothers.[112] (Such early infantile depressions were also reported by British psychoanalyst Melanie Klein[89, 90] and, in this country, by David Levy[97] over a decade ago, and by René Spitz.[163])

Babies, being very sensitive to change, are quite susceptible to depression in the first year of life. It is hard for them to adapt to new people and strange surroundings. Psychoanalytically, they are also undergoing crucial conflicts in separating psychologically from the oneness with the mother and in their beginning individuation.[104] This period may be fraught with anxieties, envies, rages, and depressions. This early phase of the start of independence and autonomy must be carried out in an atmosphere of love, care, and all the good offices of loving parents.

Meierhofer filmed five hundred babies in Zurich nurseries in order to learn to identify depression rapidly and accurately. She pinpointed certain characteristic symptoms. The main ones were a low level of activity, apathy, and a typical facial expression consisting of compressed lips and oftentimes a wrinkled forehead. These children frequently cry and cover their eyes when they are approached. These children are terribly "patient"; normal children are notoriously impatient. As very young children find it difficult to communicate with language, it is important that depression be recognized even with the lack of words.[112]

Depression in the first months of life is almost exclusively due to isolation, but isolation means more than just physical separation. These babies do not get the warm contact they need, even at their mother's side, because the parent is often ambivalent. Up to six or seven months, infants can be diverted and distracted from an episode of depression in a short time, if it is recognized. But as they approach two years of age, they are in danger of becoming resigned and may remain in a depressed state more or less permanently. By the age of three, their chances of developing a lifelong depressive neurosis are very strong. These children remain undeveloped in speech, motor activity, and adaptive behavior. They perform in mechanical ways, even when they are in groups.

In treating such cases, what does the psychiatrist do? It is essential to bring the child back to the time when he should have been given essential need-fulfilling attention and affection—in other words, proper "babying." The mother should be instructed to indulge the child's every desire, giving him her undivided attention. Eventually, she then begins to introduce the child to activities and interests appropriate to his own age level.

Dr. Meierhofer warns: "Socialist countries, and some western ones, in which children have been herded in nurseries at an early age while their mothers work, are beginning to

see the fundamental error in their system of child care."[112]
The psychoanalyst would say that women and mothers must
stop kidding themselves. Self-fulfillment for a woman must
and can be achieved without detriment to the family and
the growing child; otherwise it is just another form of victimization. Any other answer leads to social chaos.

Furthermore, there will be attendant conscious and unconscious guilt if women neglect their children or if this
faulty day-care method is practiced nationwide. This guilt
and the need to repress it will lead to wholesale distortion
and widespread social mismanagement, from which first the
children and then all of us will suffer. The guilt "has to be
denied with the aid of a delusion that things will work out
for the child anyhow, or that the precious time working
mothers spend with their child has magical properties that
the time of ordinary mothers does not have. These mothers
are always boasting about how well adjusted their children
are when often the reverse is obvious to the most untrained
eye. . . . It would be asking too much to expect that our
society, including feminists, would heed the demonstrated
truths of psychology about this issue when it is being urged
on, by the culture as a whole, to bigger and better ways of
'self-fulfillment.' "[83]

Let there be no mistake. What is involved here is a serious
and disastrous hypothesis: that the maternal role can be
neglected or can be delegated. As Abram Kardiner, quoted
above, points out, many unwary women, not directly involved with the movement but increasingly impressed with
it, may choose to endure a little guilt rather than to abandon
claims to "individuality and self-validation."[83] But men and
women should realize that they really are in the same boat
together. Both sexes are victims of the same social forces.
The real battle should not be against each other or against
children, but against the forces which destroy and erode the
lives of each individual member of the family. What they
must unite against are the false ideas which conspire to destroy the value of the male and female sexual roles. Now is
the time to bring to maternity the prestige to which it is en-

titled and which it has never been truly accorded. Just as a
mother is more than a "madonna," so she is more than a
caretaker. Motherhood is a thinking, feeling, responsible
state—and to a woman who accepts it as *part* of her life, *part*
of her fulfillment, it can be uniquely rewarding.

## The Tyranny of Equality

If any group has been "liberated," it is the women of Sweden—that is, if theirs is one's concept of freedom. Before we
completely scuttle our evolved institutions of courtship, marriage, child care, and established roles of men and women,
we should look northward to this country whose sympathies
and culture have long borne an unmistakable resemblance
to our own.

In its dedicated attempt to make "equality" a fact, the
Swedish government decided that an improvement in the
status of women could not be attained by special measures
aimed at them alone, but that it was equally necessary to
abolish conditions which gave or assigned certain privileges
and obligations or rights to *men* only. It was therefore declared that no decisive change in the distribution of "functions and status as between the sexes can be achieved if the
duties of the male in society are assumed *a priori* to be unaltered. . . . The aim of reform . . . must be to change
the traditional division of labor which tends to deprive
women of the possibility of exercising their legal rights on
equal terms."[167]

Men and women in the Swedish family were thus extended the same practical opportunity of participating in
both parenthood and gainful employment. For women to
attain positions in society outside the home, stated the law,
Swedish men would be *required* to assume a greater share
of responsibility for the upbringing of children and house-
hold chores: "A policy which attempts to give women an
equal place with men in economic life, while at the same
time confirming women's traditional responsibility for the

care of the home and children, has no prospect for fulfilling
the first of these aims."[167] Women were no longer to be economically supported in marriage, as such support would be
in direct opposition to their achieving economic independence and in direct opposition to belief in their ability to
compete on equal terms in the labor market. Similarly, the
husband's traditional obligation to support his wife was
modified to constitute a shared responsibility with her for
the support of the children. This brought about a crucial
alteration in the institution of marriage and in the meaning
of economic dependence in marriage.

When the Swedish government asserts that the new status
of men and women may appear revolutionary and unrealistic to other countries, it understates the case.

Although the women of Sweden are reluctant to admit,
because of the deep psychological consequences, that they
in fact now depend in the last analysis on the state rather
than on their husbands, such is nonetheless the case. This
new dependency is a profound disruption of the important
affective relationship which normally exists between male
and female, a love relationship with various aspects which
become intertwined and admixed during marriage: romantic love, dependency love, parental love, and sensual love
develop in a one-to-one relationship which brooks no inter-
ference by any third party. Not only youth and marriage,
but middle age and the later years are profoundly altered as
regards one's relationships and one's self-esteem if there is
no interdependency between the marital partners.

The term "male emancipation" was coined in Sweden "to
denote the right of the husband to remain at home while the
children are small, where it is found more appropriate for
the mother to devote herself to gainful employment."[167] In
actuality, such emancipation is a new division of labor under
the guise of giving men the equal right to share in the work
at home. It is a diversion in order to make the new power
structure more palatable to some men, and it is the child
who suffers by the new arrangement.

Throughout the Swedish experiment, the children are

largely reared in day-care centers by individuals who are
not their parents. Although the children are given proper
care by trained personnel, the psychiatrist cannot minimize
the effects on the child caused by loss of the unique mother-
child unit with its emotional interchange and highly indi-
vidualized mutuality and sensitivity to personal feelings. Just
as the child remains psychologically a part of the mother
for the first two to three years of life, so does he continually
need her throughout childhood for healthy emotional mat-
uration and the enhancement of the concept of self. The
range of cues and signals between mother and child occur
not only at conscious but unconscious levels. No surrogate,
however dedicated, can interpret and assimilate the myriad
messages from the child in comparable depth unless the
former were to replace the mother completely, say by adoption. The end result for the child is very likely to be one of
affective deprivation wherein optimal development of the
social emotions, especially in the area of later intimate relationships, has been compromised.

In my view, the Swedish position further collapses when
their spokesmen turn to matters of psychic health and/or
illness to buttress their arguments. For example, they assert
that "the demand for male emancipation in family life" is
supported "by the results of recent psychological research"
which has proven that the "identification of growing boys
may become uncertain and one-sided in a mother-*dominated*
home environment."[167] [Italics added]

This is a serious error on the part of the Swedish Commission. In my clinical experience, the boy's sense of identity is
damaged almost entirely when the mother is crushing psychologically and does not allow him to develop his autonomy. The father's importance is to further a process of
identification which is made possible by a mother's being
loving and encouraging, and allowing the son to be healthily
independent and autonomous from her without experiencing
fear of her disapproval. The "crushing" mother will exert the
same destructive influence whether or not she is employed

outside the home. Reducing her presence, in the immediate home environment of the child, would not necessarily reduce her virulent influence on him. To postulate that positive masculine identification is assured if the mother is away from home and the father takes care of the children is woefully erroneous.

A case in point from my clinical practice is that of a boy who was cared for by his alcoholic father from the age of one while the mother worked regularly to support the family. During her absence the father did not feel threatened by her, unlike the boy, who feared her at all times. The father abstained from drinking while she was away; immediately upon her return each evening he would very quickly become intoxicated. The son was terrified of his domineering and destructive mother and later suffered from overt homosexuality. His symptoms were directly related to his frightening mother, despite her having been away during the day.

It is an oversimplification to assume that psychopathology is caused merely by the absence and/or presence of the paternal figure. In the United States during World War II, there were many homes in which the father was away for a year or so, often for two or three years, and this did not necessarily result in the son's impaired mental health or faulty identity-formation if the mother allowed the child the freedom to grow into a separate individual and encouraged his masculine independence from her.

From the point of view of social and economic engineering, the Swedish system is impressive; from the human point of view, it may prove disastrous. Adequate medical care, social security, and educational facilities for all citizens are farsighted and humane measures which can only be applauded. That this progressive social legislation is interpreted to signify that the wife's dependency on her husband is unnecessary is a far-fetched conclusion which is beginning to prove destructive to the strength of Swedish family life.

What the system lacks is recognition of the paramount importance of the social emotions (joy, love, tenderness). It does not heed the psychodynamic laws governing mating and marriage relationships. In reality, the value of marriage is not based merely on broad social practices; it is an intricate reciprocal association in which both partners share a total commitment. If the mate relationship is regarded simply as mechanistic, with the husband and wife concerned primarily with legal (equal or not) prerogatives, and feeling only incidentally responsible for each other's well-being, the complementary and emotionally supportive nature of healthy man-woman exchange is damaged.

As a psychoanalyst, I question the extremes of the Swedish experiment which in the service of making things "equal" obliterates important and essential natural human differences. For all is not tranquil in the Eden of the North. One significant proof of serious national implication is the famous suicide rate. In 1966 it was reported at 20 per 100,-000 population, approximately twice that of the United States. Dr. Herbert Hendin, a psychoanalyst and author of *Suicide and Scandinavia*,[65] cited the suicide rate of the Swedish female at approximately 7.5 per 100,000, one-and-a-half times the comparable rate (5 per 100,000) in the United States.

Dr. Hendin, who spent years studying the Scandinavian culture at first hand, feels that he has isolated certain factors which are responsible for this alarming finding. For example, he states that the child's early separation from the mother stimulates anger and at the same time deflates self-esteem. "The control over anger and other strong emotions requires that anger be handled with a great deal of detachment. Few combinations provide such fertile soil for suicide as affective deadening combined with and paced to the need to control aggression. In the male, competitive performance is an acceptable salve for his self-esteem and may serve as an outlet for his aggression if he can so channel it. Because of rigid expectations for his own performance, however, the man becomes vulnerable to self-hatred and suicide if he fails in this area."[65]

Hendin adds that in the female, greater affectivity serves as a protective device. "Although likewise damaged by early separation from the mother, the woman's self-esteem can be restored by a stable relationship with the man if properly handled." However, her low "self-esteem is not particularly helpful in arousing and sustaining the man's interest in her."

In both men and women, therefore, "whenever the injury from the maternal relationship is more severe or the reaction to it more profound, an active paranoid attachment to the mother may become more important than any tie to work or to the opposite sex. In such circumstances, suicide often represents a destructive act aimed at both the patient and his mother."[65]

Sweden is engaged in building more and more nursery day-care centers for children of working mothers who want to resume employment as soon as possible following childbirth. The government is responding to the needs and pressures of its impatient women for increased facilities by publishing a rush of books and periodicals reinforcing what is in reality the catastrophic concept that freedom for women in Sweden includes legitimate freedom from having to raise one's own children.

By mid-1972, Swedish women had accepted "as a matter of course that they will be earning wages through a great part of their lives. The woman's greater economic independence without doubt [contributes] to the fact that she finds traditional marriage repugnant and consequently also opposes such a marriage."[69] The decline in Swedish marriages has been documented by Erland Hofsten, head of the state statistical bureau, Stockholm, Sweden. From a high point of 61,101 marriages in 1966, the number tumbled to 39,000 in 1971—a 35% drop within five years, and the lowest figures in more than a century. The decrease in marriage is most significant between the ages of 23 and 24 for women and 25 and 26 for men. Illegitimacy rose from 10 percent of all births in 1960 to 18 percent in 1970, a record figure. More and more couples have decided simply to live together.

## *The Brave New World of Margaret Mead*

The future of the family is under attack on many fronts. Margaret Mead, the mother of modern social anthropology, to whom we are indebted for many valuable cross-cultural studies of social and sexual customs, is an exponent of many of the most radical views on the future of the family. Her contention is that the current style of family organization has been a "massive failure." It may come as a surprise to many that she feels that the family as an institution has been responsible for just about every ill imaginable: adolescent rebellion cults, homosexuality, promiscuity, alcoholism, drug addiction, and psychosomatic disorders. The cause of all these, she believes, is the emphasis on exclusive dependence on a single mate and on parenthood.[110]

By the year 2000, if not sooner, according to Mead, these cultural disasters will have turned around. Her new world will emerge out of the population crisis, as she puts it, as a response to the "world situation." She predicts that the end result will be "a new willingness to assume responsibility for supporting massive dependence on modern scientific methods for the control of conception, artificial insemination, artificial lactation, and extra-uterine gestation. A new type of family unit will appear, with a high tolerance of childless marriage, and in which parenthood would be limited to a smaller number of families whose principle function would be child-rearing. . . . The rest of the population would be free to function for the first time in history—as individuals."[110] The implication is that individuals have not hitherto functioned as such—an idea that would be puzzling to philosophers from Plato through the Renaissance and to the present day. But this reinvention of history is part of the current phenomenon.

One can readily agree with Mead's hopeful statements that in her new world boys and girls will have a similar education and like demands will be made on them for citizenship, economic contribution, and creativity. Security will be provided to those in dependent positions by reason of lack of education or physical disability, mental and physical illness, or old age. There would be no limitation on freedom for women as a social group. While one agrees with her idea of a good relationship as one in which companionship for "work, play and stable living would decide relationships," one is nonetheless astonished by her assertion that boys and girls would be differentiated not by sex-type personality characteristics, but by temperament, whatever that means. *The two-sex exclusive pair model of human relationships would thus lose its power.*

Mead warns that society may not give up its old ways easily, and that changes in the basic social style of interpersonal relations and sex-defined roles which now exist might well engender a "counter-revolution." The counter-revolutionists' aim will be to "refocus attention on the home, limit sexual freedom, curtail the individual development of women, subordinate the creative capacities of the individual adult to the needs of the group for docile parents, workers and citizens."[110]

Revolutionary blueprints must, of course, include means of dealing with dissenters, and Mead's is no exception. For example, she believes that "social protection" must be instituted for both men and women during the transition stages in the development of the new style of behavior and the new role of sex. Women must be provided with socially responsible protection during the period when old forms, based on male responsibility, are becoming outmoded. She rightly complains that, as yet, new arrangements that will support women's freedom to earn and to function as independent individuals have not been realized on a very large scale. If, however, this isn't done, she warns, the conscience of the community may well be aroused against the ever-increasing number of motherless homes, homes abandoned by women who are determined to proceed on their own. This may well tend to support the superiority of the older, traditionally sanctioned, forms of social organization.[110]

Her idea of revolution is a cold and bleak portrayal of

what will happen to men and women, sons and daughters, should her predictions become reality. While she herself feels that a weakening in the sense of sex identity in men may then make itself felt in the exploits of adolescent gangs, protest groups, in fads expressed in styles of dress and special treatment of the body, she yet has a cure for everything. Since a man's sense of sexual identity will no longer be provided him by "social differences" which will no longer exist, attention should be given to the vicissitudes of this transitional phase so that men "do not suffer too much." (!) Her suggested treatment is that sexual identity for boys will be provided by a form of sex education which emphasizes feats of skill, strength, and bravery.[110]

The psychoanalyst knows only too well that these exercises in themselves cannot produce a sense of sexual identity in anyone. They are merely a small part of masculine identity which actually depends most upon influences experienced in the first three years of life—influences arising from proper mothering. Man's development of sexual identity occurs when he successfully traverses the separation-individuation phase of human development, normally by the age of three. This is an *intrapsychic* development which is dependent upon the mother's lovingly and caringly allowing the child to become free of her, form his own identity, while she (on her side) helps, abets, encourages, his strength, independence, and masculinity, as differentiated from her own feminine identity, thereby supporting the boy's efforts to become truly an individual entity, separate and different from herself.

Mead makes the crucial mistake of looking at differences between masculinity and femininity as if they can be "attributed largely to differences in upbringing, the female proceeding by direct identification with a neutering parent, and the male by differentiation from the neutering parent."[110]

She incorrectly believes that when men and women are equally involved in domestic or family life in terms of the same activities, there will be a marked emphasis on indi-

viduality. What she desires is a "reduction in sex-based differences, in mental attitudes." She states that such an outcome is "predictable, not only as one result of changed styles
of education for boys and girls, but also as one effect of
the biochemical dampening of female rhythms."[110] In effect,
she announces as a "happy" result (contrary to all physiological knowledge) that even hormones will change.

Mead's revolutionary new world is essentially a world of
growing disregard for sex as the basic mode of differentiation between men and women. The two-sex exclusive-pair
model of human relationships would lose its power and disappear at least, that is her prophesy and hope.

Mead has long held a position of authority as one of
America's leading social scientists. As a person, she is gentle
in manner and persuasive in speech. But she is not qualified
to make pronouncements in the field of conscious and unconscious psychodynamics and early psychosexual development. My disagreement with and opposition to her "sexual
revolution" is evident in the foregoing chapters of this book.

There are other sources of criticism of some of Mead's
conclusions, however. The general confusion of her writings
on sex, sexual identity, and the differences between the
sexes—as distinct from her other brilliant work—has been
nowhere better illuminated than in *Sexuality and Homosexuality* by Arno Karlen.[85] Karlen, a journalist, a researcher
in sex, its history, and development over the centuries, asserts that Mead's book, *Sex and Temperament*, was the "beginning of the misunderstanding." She attempted then to
prove that sex role is *socially* learned to a great degree and
varies from society to society. Furthermore, masculine and
feminine are not simply opposite, nor are they strictly equivalent to dominance or passivity. Sex role may involve anything from occupation to posture and choice of language.
According to Karlen, "Much of educated America and of
the educated West was ready to hear the idea that traditional sex roles aren't necessarily natural or good—and to accept the feminine bias with which Mead presented it."[85]

The subliminal message of her writing, according to Columbia anthropologist Ralph Linton (as reported by Karlen), was that

> There were no significant differences between the sexes or at least only such differences as would inspire envy in the male. Mead believed that sex role, despite its complex interplay with constitution, is purely a social convention. She avoided dwelling on even basic anatomical sex differences; ignoring that humans are mammals, she said it is just more "convenient" for women than men to raise children. Like most feminists, she directly or indirectly praised lack of aggression in men and assertiveness in women: she found redeeming virtues in Mundugumor males, but few in Arapesh "big men."[109] Most important she claimed the specialized, contrasting sex roles create deviance and neuroticism. In fact, there is no such evidence that deviance and neuroticism arise from such fanciful sources.

Then, resuming his own critique, Karlen continues:

> Mead viewed sex role distinctions a priori as a burden or psychological imprisonment. To a gifted woman such as herself, they might be. But she failed to point out that when society makes a demand, it doesn't just punish those who fail to meet it; it also rewards and supports those who live up to it. In later years,[111] Mead somewhat corrected the bias in her work, saying that the sexes tend to have different gifts to cultivate. She still makes such statements, however, that show glee over female aggression and a superiority and pity for males.[85]

# Chapter 4

# GROUP SEX

### The Beast with Two (or More) Backs

Shakespeare's "beast with two backs" has become the beast with three, four, five, and more backs, bosoms, genitals, and other anatomical features—the components of group sex *and* its accompanying psychodynamics. Stripped of the intellectual process of objective thought as well as the social emotions of love, tenderness, and pride, man emulates the beast of prey and of brute "emotion" in these forays. The irony is that most participants in group sex are, in reality, not so "sexy"; they usually suffer from a variety of sexual inhibitions and disorders.

It is estimated that perhaps one to two million adults in the United States engage in group sex each year. Enthusiasts for this new sexual custom proclaim that it is simply a safety valve for the benefit of our culture. On the contrary, viewed objectively, it is a sign that the culture is in deep trouble. When a society fails in great measure to meet the needs of its citizens in terms of both social role and just rewards, there is always a rise in homicide, delinquency, homosexuality, and promiscuity. Group sex is one variety of promiscuity, and far from being an innovation it goes back to antiquity, to other times in history when people no longer wished to control their instinctual impulses.

The phenomenon of group sex arises out of the destruction of traditional parent-child roles. Responsibility for exemplifying healthy man-woman relationships no longer abides with the parents; adults no longer feel that they have to conduct themselves according to traditional values. They simply "cop out" on image, identity, and example-setting, without examining either their reasons for doing so or the possible consequences of such an act. Profound feelings of emptiness lead men and women to search for meaning in order to overcome the absence of a sense of self and alleviate deep frustration. It is almost as if orgasm with multiple partners is expected to provide a panacea, emptiness replaced by a crowd—and what a lonely crowd it is.[62]

Group sex signifies too a loss of idealization of a preferred partner. It emerges from a decimation of the importance of the family and the misused freedom of modern contraceptive techniques.

It is the female who is most grossly exploited in group sex. In times of social crisis men tend to become markedly hostile toward women. They are afraid of failing to meet the demands they feel women make on them, yet they know they cannot do without women. They misuse women under the pretext that group sex is a part of "female liberation," with as many orgasms as possible for everyone. In this deception the victim is the female, although ultimately the man is his own victim as well. The activities of group sex are a dramatization of the polymorphous-perverse phase of childhood, ordinarily renounced around the age of four or five, when voyeuristic, exhibitionistic, and homosexual experimentation are abandoned. Group sex is part and parcel of the threatened destruction of sex.

Who gets involved in group sex? Anyone who desires extra sexual "kicks," extra thrills, surplus variation, anyone who has the personality components required to continue this practice beyond perhaps one brief trial. It is often simply an attempt to sanction extramarital experiences without emotional involvement. Some people apparently engage in group sex because of an overwhelming sense of boredom with their lives and themselves. Others have no conception of what love in sex or sex in love are all about; if they cannot have it, why not destroy it? The sour-grapes principle applies. Some use group sex hoping that it will prove to be an aphrodisiac for their potency difficulties. Men will do almost anything to try to hide the fact of impotence both from themselves and from others. Some may rationalize their behavior by saying they are "democratizing" sex. There are men and women who profit financially by arranging group-sex parties and by publishing lists of available couples. But the overall purpose is orgastic experience, without emotional or social responsibility, particularly when the restraining mechanism of conscience can be extinguished through the familiar "sharing of the guilt" mechanism.

Clinically, chronic "group sexers" are likely to reveal a failure of warm, affectionate, sensual relationships with the opposite sex. Many of them suffer from sexual inhibitions in one-to-one relationships from which they hope to free themselves in the group setting. There is a progressive dehumanization of sex itself; variational sexual practices, which predominate in these gatherings, devoid of all significant interpersonal communication in other spheres of activity, destroy any residue of or potential for tender affectivity and emotional relatedness.

One "gains" orgasms in group sex but only with great emotional deprivation. In addition to missing the vital components of tenderness and love, the individual can derive no sense of personal pride and self-esteem from these contacts, feelings so important to life itself.

The self can be adequately nourished only by acts which produce genuine pride and feelings of self-worth; if not thus nurtured, the self dwindles and gradually withers away. The barren mechanical release of sexual instinctual drives leaves one empty after the few seconds of orgasm. Real sex and sexuality are cheated, and life is cheapened. The aim of healthy sexual relations is completely subverted, for a paramount function of sex is to bring two individuals closer together.

Group sex has nothing to do with love. It is not more love, as its proponents claim;[7, 105] it is less love—no love at all. In fact, the "cardinal sin" in group sex is to become emotionally involved with any partner. Aldous Huxley, in *Point Counterpoint* (1928) and *Brave New World* (1932), was the first to predict that the sexual code of the future may well be one of total promiscuity, its only taboo that of stable, long, meaningful love relationships.

Once a sexual custom is established, society usually pays no attention to it. The belief is that if it is not a socially expedient and useful custom, its defects will soon be manifest and people will cry out. But people do not always know where the hurt comes from. The trail has been lost; many harmful customs escape detection as sources of human misery because their effects are concealed and ignored at the outset. The outset of social deterioration appears to be now; the real nature of newly established sexual customs must be recognized before it is too late.

# Chapter 5

# COMMUNAL LIVING

Communes are not new. They were present in revolutionary Moscow a half-century ago, and in utopian communities throughout the world long before that. As Ralph Blumenthal pointed out in a 1968 article, their basic purpose was to foster "super families . . . cells of the new sexual and social order . . . to launch revolutionary assault on what the radicals regard as an encrusted and smug society."[17]

Their main goal is political and social change; thus sexual liberation and living together in groups is mostly a means to an end. Simultaneously, communes often seek to destroy the social and sexual structure that currently exists between men and women by flaunting the multiple sexual relations and license between members of the group. These individuals are "convinced that a revolution in the streets demands a revolution in the bedroom. . . ."

Blumenthal classifies such experiments into three general types. First, the hard-core radical communes in which "all property and bodies are theoretically held in common and privacy is despised." The second comprises "more moderate forms of bisexual apartment sharing, mostly by students. Here the members have their own belongings and private lives, but seek the economic, social and political advantages of group living." The third type is the "student village," in which almost all of the students live in "domestic tranquility in sexual-integrated dormitories." There appears to be a difference between radical experiments in theory from the hedonistic communal living of the American hippies as compared with those of the political communards of Berlin in the 1960s. The Americans try more to combine political and sexual underpinnings.

Americans seem not so aware of the political and social implications of their sexual-liberation communards. They feel that one can also seek out solutions to personal needs simultaneously with political action. Some of the causes espoused by these groups are anti-fascism, pro-Maoist China, black power, anti-junta-dominated Greece, as well as opposition to the Vietnam war. There is a "keen sense of the absurd in modern life and admiration for the dadaist tactics of provocateurs."[17] These acts of provocation involve engaging in disorderly conduct. For example, individuals have calmly pulled their trousers down in court before approaching the bench, defecated on the lawyer's table, and wiped themselves with pages for the trial document. At a congressional hearing, one of the youthful militants approached the dais and hurled a large cream pie into the face of the chairman. Communes are often seen by their inhabitants to be part of rebellion against society.

Members of the communards do not know what kind of society they want to make; they simply state that they would like to fight against the old, destroy it, and be ready for the new society when it takes over, whatever it is, whenever it is.

All group living seems to founder on the problem of sex, that is group sex. After espousing the ideal that a person should sleep with whomever he wants, communal groups have found that there are nights of "terror" in which one particular person will come home to find his or her partner making love to someone else. Modifications have been tried. For instance, a kind of live-in community in large apartments by groups of young people—sometimes in couples, sometimes unattached—may be introduced. This group may have its own finances, may own property collectively and may guard its group privacy, and may share the social and

political advantages of shared expenses, mutual companionship, and shared political activity. But importantly, they do
not trade sexual partners.

Usually it is the female in such a situation who becomes
jealous and does not wish to share with other women the
protection afforded her by a particular man. Men with a
borderline or frail heterosexual orientation tend to develop
pathological jealousy or even paranoiac symptoms. Men who
unconsciously perceive rejection by a female to be a form
of castration are likely to become extremely vengeful. All
in all, sexuality is a strong master, not easily cheapened or
weakened in its expression without major complications.

A theologian might put it this way: that God in His infinite wisdom has not left the satisfaction of the sexual instinct simply to caprice but equips man with the faculty of
choice and the certainty of consequences whether from the
torments of his own conscience or the reprisal of his fellow-
men. A psychiatrist would formulate it another way: that
man is prevented by the built-in presence of emotions from
degrading his potential of greatest joy to merely an unbridled
dled mechanistic foray. Such sexual exploitation of everyone
who may be vulnerable enough or naïve enough to regard
his sexual use as liberation ultimately deprives sexual activities of meaning and value and often penalizes the exploiter
with psychic disturbances manifested by impotence and
frigidity.

Sexual life fulfills itself best in an atmosphere of tenderness, delight, and deep affectivity. When these components
are absent, severe aggression, boredom, and tedium may
suffuse all of living. The commune cannot escape instinct's
stringent demands.

Those who engage in communal living claim that they
alone are not "hung up" on sex. To them it is simply another
sensory experience to be readily available when desired, a
commodity like eggs or detergent. What a contradiction in
terms! The very mention of the need for "plenty of sex" implies a state of sexual hunger which is then satisfied. The
communal inhabitants insist that since sex is always avail-

able, it will no longer be of consuming interest; that is, it will not constitute a major motivational force in their lives. Such a conclusion is fallacious in the extreme, as it is unlikely that the more accessible sex is, the more it will "cool down," except for the brief period of time required to build up new sexual tensions and energies heightened by grossly enlarged opportunities.

When it is no longer important to adapt as male or female, sex, according to some communes, will be "freer but less important." The tantalizing suggestion is hard to miss—free sex, free "love," is to be had for the asking. This laissez faire attitude toward sexual identity is then rationalized on grounds that it is undemocratic to insist that one is either masculine or feminine: sexuality is thus first abused and then denied.

*Chapter 6*

# PORNOGRAPHY:
# THE RAPE OF THE SENSES

## *Definition of Pornography*

D. H. Lawrence probably gave the best definition of pornography: "You can recognize [it] by the insult offered, invariably, to sex and to the human spirit . . . , the insult to the human body, the insult to a vital human relationship!"[95]

Journalist Pete Hamill puts it this way: "Women in these books and magazines are not living human beings: they are canisters of flesh, to be whipped, chained, raped, burned with cigarettes, stepped on, or whatever vile act the writers can imagine. These are not women with intelligence, with hopes, with fears or complicated desires; they are fantasies for people who think happiness is somehow involved with a succession of accessible vaginas, lacerated flesh, or the infliction of violence. . . . It might be an amusing intellectual conceit for the literary critics; but the mallet-headed high school dropout who reads that book and thinks that it is a description of what women want is a man who might commit a crime, privately or publicly; the crime, of course, is the violation of another human being."[63]

Furthermore, Hamill warns that we are "growing more inhuman and grimy day by day, and the pornography wave is only a part of it. . . . [If we] continue to fill up our growing emptiness with rotten fantasies, the result will be a state even more murderous and malignant than the one we have now, if this is possible."

In order to avoid false moralizing as regards normal and healthy sexual functioning, sexual activities can be divided or classified scientifically into those occurring as *modified* or as *standard* patterns of sexual arousal and orgasm. Pornography may be used by those belonging to either group but is more likely to appear frequently in those with modified patterns.

Characteristic of the sex experience is, first of all, that the sexual act takes place between a male and a female. Orgasm is produced by entry of the penis into the vagina. There is a tendency for a commingling of pleasures—for example, oral-genital activities with other sensory modalities. Touching, kissing, looking, are all aimed at heightening the volume of excitation preliminary to orgasm. Acts of defecation and urination do not usually take place as part of this sexually pleasurable activity. Aggression, sadism, anger, fear, rage, pain, hatred, grief—the emergency emotions of the organism —are conspicuously absent. Their introduction into the sexual motive state normally *decreases* or eliminates sexual pleasure. The presence of love, joy, and tenderness *increases* the pleasure of the experience.

Those who can achieve orgasm *only and invariably* in the absence of an adult partner of the opposite sex, or only if there is *no* penetration of the male organ into the female, suffer from a disturbance of sexual functioning. In addition, there are some borderline individuals who may be able to perform with a partner of the opposite sex only in an emotional climate of hate, rage, and aggression. These persons are so frightened by their fears of sex that they must mobilize their defiant rage to overcome the inhibiting action of their fear. Both kinds of sexual performance—the one without penetration, the other in a hostile mood—are considered disturbed.

We are born into a cultural matrix which in interaction with our mammalian heritage produces the standard male-female coital pattern. Within this pattern, of course, there are multiple healthy individual variations of sexual arousal and expression. These healthy patterns comprise the gamut of personal experience and psychological preference. Because the possibilities for pleasure are bountiful, no one can logically claim that "normal" sex is boring sex.

Truly responsible individuals in many communities are at a loss as to what to do about pornography/obscenity. For example, some earnest residents of a town of 30,000 in the midwestern United States banded together in August of 1970 to form a Concerned Community Citizens Committee in order to stem the inundation of their movie theaters and magazine stands with pornography. But they were stalled when they were unable to define pornography, and ended their project by deciding not to try. By doing so, they defeated their own purpose. Being "fair-minded people," their ranks were scattered by the rationalization that there were "more serious problems" in their city demanding attention, and they were rendered completely ineffectual by the accusation that they were treading on the freedom of others through the threatened imposition of "censorship."

But why is the issue of pornography so difficult to understand? The word itself is a misnomer, as it is derived from the Greek *porne* and *graphos*, literally meaning "writing about whores." Obscenity comes from the Latin for "filthy" or "repulsive" and is much closer to the point. In legal language, when pornography is preceded by the term "hardcore," it is meant to be interchangeable with the word "obscenity."

Pornography can be divided into writings on the one hand and pictorial representation on the other; the latter might better be termed pornology except for the common usage of the word pornography to designate both. Hard-core pornography should be separated from other types of literature with erotic content or subject matter that differs in certain essential qualities from pornography. The latter is termed *erotic realism*. By using such terminology, both pornography and erotic fiction and non-fiction can be classified and differentiated.

There is no valid objection to erotic pictorial art. This material emphasizes the emotional and the aesthetic, not the physiological sex responses. It docs not inflict upon sex the grossly destructive negative impact of pornography. Rembrandt's nudes, Picasso's erotic drawings, as well as *Lady Chatterly's Lover* and other honest and insightful literary works, are examples of erotic realism.

At times erotic realism may produce some physiological sexual reaction in the spectator. We do not have clear-cut and definite answers as to whether the artist who paints or writes erotically is motivated by desires to stimulate *physiological* responses in his viewers or readers—probably he does not. The pornographer always does; this is his major motive. Erotic or sexual *responses* are not what make a piece of work pornographic, however—*intention* does.

According to the findings of the Kronhausens, a husband-wife team who have completed extensive research on the development of pornography, "The basic difference between erotic realism and pornography lies in the different approach in handling the problem of reality. . . . In contrast to erotic realism, pornography is not concerned with reality at all, but sets aside all considerations of reality in favor of the wish-fulfilling fantasies of its 'predominantly male' authors and anticipated reactions of predominantly male readership."[92]

It is not the appeal to sexuality or the production of sexual reactions which renders an object pornographic. It is not even merely the intention to arouse sexual feelings on the part of the author, artist, or photographer. There is nothing wrong with experiencing sexual arousal in response to any erotic stimulus. As D. H. Lawrence said, "The right sort of sex stimulus . . . is invaluable to human daily life . . . without which 'the world grows grey.'" But it is the wish and will to do "dirt on sex" which makes a thing pornographic. As Lawrence astutely noted, "As soon as there is sex excitement with the desire to spite the sexual feeling, to humiliate it and degrade it, the element of pornography enters."[95]

Pornography is widely available in our society today.

When I scan the vast number of titles of pornographic books at a neighborhood luncheonette in uptown Manhattan, I am continually struck, at times almost humorously, by the analogy between pornography and other forms of unreal living, such as soap operas. Pornography is vicarious living; it is an activity enjoyed through identification with some other person. Both have to do with unreal situations, and both are dishonest. Pornography parodies emotional life just as soap operas simplify and distort social and domestic life. While both may provide temporary kicks or thrills, they in fact parody real life. While illicit activities are subject to fear and shame in the "soaps," they nevertheless are used to stimulate, titillate, and retain the interest of the audience.

Thus, what is vital to our comprehension of pornography is not that it arouses sexual feelings. Many of the greatest paintings, pictures, music, films, are great precisely because of their sexual appeal. The Titians, Renoirs, Matisses, Michelangelos, the Song of Solomon, are great because, as Lawrence said, "the loveliness is all interwoven with sex appeal, sex stimulus. . . . Michelangelo . . . can't help filling the Cornucopia with phallic acorns." Because sex is a powerful, beneficial, and necessary stimulus in human life, he says rightly, we are "grateful when we feel its warm, natural flow, like a form of sunshine."[95]

Here we have our definition: *when sexual excitement is mixed with the desire to humiliate, to degrade, or to befoul —the very element which makes up pornography has been introduced.*

Pornography is not the nude or semi-nude pin-up girls which adorned the walls of men away from women during World War II, or the displays of nudity in *Playboy* magazine. Pin-ups serve as a temporary satisfaction, through wishful thinking, as a substitute for anticipated sex. For the most part they are a dramatization of wholesome sex. But the pictorialization of sex in pornography is a degradation, as for example in the centerfold of *Screw*, where a woman's sexual organs appear, gaping, legs held wide apart by two nude muscle men. The idea is to excite the viewer by por-

traying a female victimized—excitement is thus equated
with exploiting both reader and subject.

## Types of Pornography

Pornography ranges from the mildly suggestive to the
absurdly exaggerated. Recurring themes can be summed up
as incest, seductive parental figures, a profaning of the
sacred, "supersexed" males, "nymphomaniac" females, homosexuality (especially lesbian activities), scenes of flagellation
in the context of sexual relations, the sexual abuse of individuals who are seen as "low caste" such as blacks, and
foreigners, the use of children and animals in sex relations.
These constitute almost the entire arsenal of the pornographer. One is hard put to find a significant variation from
these stereotypes which, in themselves, are identifying characteristics of pornography. The suggestions offered by pornography are dangerous to the vulnerable—to children and
indeed to all of those who suffer from childhood fears and
guilts.

Specialized types of seduction scenes are brief and frequent in pornography. The women are generally shown to
be as eager for seduction as the men. In all defloration scenes
there is usually a sadistic element. When women are portrayed as resistant to seduction, the typical story line emphasizes that the victim need not be coaxed after the initial
experience. She then participates willingly and with gusto in
abnormal sexual experimentation.

Incestuous relations are portrayed as frequent and guilt-
free. To encourage sexual relations between members of the
same family by removing the barrier of guilt is in essence to
destroy the family. The incest barrier is the product of thousands of years of evolution culminating in the family unit.
Aside from preventing inbreeding of potentially unhealthy
genetic combinations, its purpose is to promote family stability, group cohesion, and cooperation. It protects children
from sexual exploitation, adults from the overwhelming envy

of the young, and the young from a wish to destroy parental authority and seize adult sexual privilege. Freud's brilliant psychoanalytic study *Totem and Taboo* uncovered the profound unconscious significance of incest prohibitions and their vital function in preserving family life and promoting later normal healthy mental functioning.

In pornography, the sacred and profane are intermingled; these opposites are used to heighten erotic feelings. If sex is sinful, then sexual acts "committed in sacred surroundings or with the participation of representatives of religion, constitute the ultimate in blasphemy," according to the Kronhausens.[9] The use of obscene language is found on every page, and the use of formerly taboo words is frequent to the point of tedium.

The dimensions of the male genitals are exaggerated as well as the amount of seminal fluid produced in ejaculation. Psychoanalytically, it is easily deduced that the source of these distortions is the male's great fear of sexual impotence, often verbalized as a fear that his penis is too small to carry out intercourse. This fear appears regularly in the dreams of patients with sexual conflicts. Fears as to genital adequacy expressed as a concern with size are secondary to fears of castration originating in childhood. To those who harbor this painful self doubt, false reassurance is available through pornographic distortion by identifying with the more amply endowed fictive physique.

The male characters in pornographic works simulate intense sexual passion mixed with a high degree of aggression. From the clinical point of view we know that men who have become impotent lose their capacity for "push." They are unable to engage in pelvic thrusting movements easily and feel frightened, submissive, and passive in the sexual act, thus unfortunately insuring failure. Their identification with this sexually overaggressive male may so fortify them as to allow achievement of orgasm. In many men, however, the loss of normal assertiveness in the sex act leads to a wide and frantic search for erotically aggressive material. It is utilized in an attempt to find release with a female partner. The Marquis de Sade—who proceeded from cruelty to murder for "sexual kicks"—spent half his life in prison for the enactment of his pornographic fantasies. This infamous man unfortunately began acting out his impulses rather than containing them in his fantasies. Thus can pornography come alive.

Pornography exploits the myth of the black male, falsely believed to possess larger genitals than the white male—another approach intended to ward off castration fears. The myth that they are "inferior" implies that sex with blacks is a demeaning, degrading, and masochistic act. This combination of supersexuality and domination supposedly increases the consumer's excitement, and probably does if he has sexual problems.

By observing homosexual relations in pornography one can ward off fears of homosexuality and reduce guilt through the familiar sharing-of-the-guilt mechanism—and one can get rid of anxiety about possible latent homosexual impulses. In all homosexual pornography there is a decisive sadomasochistic theme; homosexual intercourse is often an expression of the deepest primitive aggressions. Almost invariably in the psychoanalysis of male homosexuals, concealed by surface defensiveness and rationalization, we hear the plaintive cry of a little boy: "How I wanted my father to love me! But now I want to punish him, to force him to give me love, to shove my penis down his throat where I can hurt him, swallow him, swallow his penis, swallow his entire body. Then he'll never be able to leave me." Homosexual material in pornography shows such fantasies acted out.

Homosexual sex represents the disarming and conquest of the father, the first male who frustrated the boy in his wishes for normal masculine paternal love and thereby deprived him of his wish to be a man. For it is by the act of loving identification with the father that the boy gains his model for masculinity. In the sexual act the homosexual obtains masculine identity from the partner, a substitute for the rejecting, hostile, or elusive father. This functions like a "shot" of masculinity. Experiencing orgastic satisfaction temporarily neutralizes the intense primitive anxieties which would otherwise disturb the psychological equilibrium of the homosexual. The act must be endlessly repeated or the anxiety states may become unbearable.

Sadomasochistic scenes, whether heterosexual or homosexual, involving psychic or bodily pain (flagellation) provide a vicarious punishment to the viewer or reader of pornography. Because users of these materials are obsessed with sadomasochism, they consciously or unconsciously believe they should be punished for sexual pleasure; through pornography they obtain license to experience an orgasm through the imaginary suffering of others.

Illusory mastery and control of the sexual partner is the trademark of pornography. This guaranteed control is necessary because the consumer of this genre completely misunderstands the meaning of sex. Pornography obliges him by supporting and fixing his semidelusional conception that in order to obtain sexual satisfaction one of the partners must have *complete* control and the other must be, in a sense, victimized. He cannot function as a partner in an activity which in fact requires a great deal of mutual cooperation to be even minimally gratifying.

Sometimes when first introduced to pornography, normal adults may experience a heightening or stimulation of erotic desire. While the sight of naked bodies or the visualization of sexual intercourse or other acts usually proves initially exciting, the effect, for most people, subsides with repetition. In *The Story of O,* for example, the girl's sexual relations with her partner are at first stimulating to many readers. But the punishment and cruelty visited upon her by her seducers, by whom she is held sexual prisoner, usually causes sexual excitement to fade. The pornography devotee must continually seek only this substitute method of achieving orgasm because he is so damaged in sexual functioning or becomes so frightened by attempting more normal sexual relations.

*Compulsive* interest in pornography is especially high among men who suffer from fears of impotence, fears of genital smallness, fears of castration. A troubling lack of spontaneous sexual need may motivate the man to artificially promote a psychological buildup of desire. Thus the use of pornography/obscenity may be preliminary to seeking actual sexual contact with a woman, or it may occur during sexual relations in order to buttress a waning or failing sexual performance. On occasion such individuals may resort to its use in the absence of a woman in order to sustain excitement during masturbation.

Underlying the chronic use of pornography is the fear of sex. Such fear arises in earliest childhood and is due to the prohibitions and intimidations by the parents or their surrogates with consequent development of anxiety, guilt, and fear in the child. Fear of sex is not of course innate; it is learned behavior which leads to adult inhibition. Upon reaching adolescence and adulthood, an inhibited person finds he is unable to function whenever he approaches a sexual situation without an accompanying measure of fear and guilt. He must find a circuitous way to circumvent these fears and simultaneously obtain sexual release. Pornography thus offers an adjunct technique to these persons in their attempt to achieve release of sexual tension. This in no way solves their problem, and indeed may make it worse as stronger and stronger doses of pornography may be required to bring about orgasm, with an ultimate failure of performance.

Some commentators on this subject feel that pornography is helpful when used by those suffering from severe sexual disorders. It is hard to believe that pornography—whether scatological, sadomasochistic, homosexual, or depicting other sexual deviations—has any therapeutic value. Nor can it successfully function as a harmless psychological release or safety valve. Deep-rooted anxieties in the unconscious mind cannot be dissipated and removed by the superficial expedient of resorting to pornographic material. Anxieties of this intensity will return until root causes are explored and treated, and any relief experienced through pornography, whether or not resulting in orgasm, is momentary, ultimately destructive to self-esteem, and entirely peripheral to the real problem.

The proponents of pornography always declare that it is not intended for children—indeed, that they are proscribed from its use. Further, they insist that there would be no adverse effect on children or family life were pornography legalized. I wonder how this argument can be seriously put forth when a substantial proportion of hard-core pornographic literature singles out children for sexual victimization and shows their exploitation as a popular theme. As of 1972, even this has changed. Many of our leading "sexologists," John Money of Johns Hopkins and several prominent others in the field, are advocating the use of pornographic films of both homosexual and heterosexual types in the sex-education courses of the young.[114]

The New York luncheonette mentioned before offers for sale a large quantity of pornographic paperbacks. All of these encourage the idea that perverse sexual practices, especially pedophilia (adult-child seduction) and incest, are prevalent and rewarding. The unrestricted purveyance of pornography (this luncheonette is a neighborhood gathering place for school children) makes it impossible realistically to safeguard children and disturbed adults from the damaging influence of such literature's emphasis on perversion as a desirable basis for all sexual relations. And perversion, rather than simply sex, is the chief selling point. Just in passing I have noted these paperback titles: *Hers Were Young: A Woman Addicted to Youth; Women and Boys— Sexual Lovers; A Girl's Best Friend* (cover depicts a dog about to perform cunnilingus on a girl approximately thirteen or fourteen); *Mama's Boy* (cover depicts a woman in black lace lingerie bathing a boy of approximately fourteen; in addition to his nudity, her buttocks are exposed); *Teacher's Pet* (cover depicts children, boys and girls about twelve, ogling the teacher's revealed breasts and partially exposed pelvic area); *School Librarian* (cover depicts a woman sitting on a high stool against a backdrop of books, legs apart, genitals fully exposed to two boys of slightly post-puberty age); *The Family* (cover depicts two adolescent girls being coached by their mother in perverse acts).


## The Strengthening Tide of Pornography

The current wave of pornography did not inundate us suddenly. It was a slowly developing stream which required nearly twenty years to arrive at these shores as a rampaging sea.

The landmark decision to allow films of pornographic content into the United States was made quite innocently in 1952 when the United States Supreme Court ruled that the New York Film Licensing Board could not deny a license to the Italian film *The Miracle* on the grounds that it was "sacrilegious." Thus the assault on our senses began apparently as a religious issue, not a sexual one. The 1952 decision was to become a Trojan Horse of the sexual revolution. It contained within it a ruling that movies were to be protected by the same constitutional guarantees afforded other mass media. The point was specifically made that nudity in itself is not obscene and that no film can be judged so unless its dominant appeal is to "prurient" interest and the entire work is without redeeming social value.

That the gates of the censorship fortress were open did not go unnoticed by foreign filmmakers and some in this country, too. A flood of obscene films was imported, and new ones, quickly and cheaply made in this country, began to be shown in small movie theaters in the larger urban areas.

A second landmark was the licensing of a bigger-budget film from Stockholm entitled *I Am Curious, Yellow,* with scenes of oral sexual relations, nudity, and sexual intercourse. The United States Supreme Court felt that this film was not "utterly without redeeming social value."

The coup de grace was delivered on September 10, 1969, when a Federal panel decision held unconstitutional a bill allowing the Postmaster General to stop mail deliveries to suspected vendors of obscene material.

These United States decisions were antedated by the one on July 1, 1969, in Denmark, which abolished the last of the legal barriers against publishing pictorial pornography and showing "blue movies." The Danes' new law added a proviso that made it an offense to sell pictorial pornography to anyone under seventeen years of age, thereby making it appear that morality and protection of the young had won the day. The authorities believed that the sale of pictorial pornography would fall sharply if there were no legal sanctions—a superb piece of rationalization. They "reasoned" that prohibition stimulates interest; therefore legitimatizing pornography would divest it of its "forbidden fruit" excitement.

They had already sold themselves a bill of goods in the case of written pornography when this was legalized in 1967. The Danes made a distinction between written and pictorial pornography, and for some unknown reason considered pictorial pornography possibly more harmful than written pornography. Both written and pictorial pornography, however, were seen to be harmful *only* to those individuals below the age of 17.

The claim that there was a decrease in sex crimes in Denmark in the late 1960s–early 1970s seems to me attributable to reasons other than the availability of pornography and obscenity. Furthermore, a decline in excess of 25 percent is a most unlikely statistic and needs more explaining. Some Danish psychiatrists say that this remarkable trend is due to the "relaxation of passions" afforded by the unrestricted use of pornographic materials, but this seems unlikely. My opinion was ultimately supported by none other than Dr. Berl Kutschinsky, a Danish criminologist-psychologist and himself the head of the 1969 Danish Pornography Study. He was quoted in *The New York Times*, November 9, 1970, as admitting that ". . . there was no direct proof that legalization of pornography was responsible for the decline in sex crimes."[93]

In my clinical judgment a flood of material describing sexual sadism, masochism, humiliation, incest, pedophilia, and other comparably damaging and dehumanizing activities would lead to *less* impulse-control and therefore to a rise in criminal acting-out. Not having personal access to the statistical samplings, I cannot determine the basis for the alleged decline in sex crimes in Denmark. However, no clarification has been offered by the Danish government officials who made this claim that would prove any connection between the sale of pornography, the incidence and seriousness of sex crimes, and the correlation between them. Heightened impulse-stimulation of an erotic nature, publicly promoted, can only serve as a force favoring explosive acts of sexual aggression rather than as a deterrent or an inhibiting agent.

We are told that following World War II, the Danish people wanted "freedom" from the power of government. In actuality, they have allowed the state new power—the influence exerted by passing new laws proclaiming pornography/ obscenity not harmful. It is interesting to note that once pornography was sanctioned, the Danes promptly relaxed all laws related to sexual behavior including those concerning homosexuality.

In 1969 the Danish Medical-Legal Council declared that pornography has no effect on vital aspects of behavior, an opinion based on simple poll-taking and one which is beyond comprehension because of its obvious superficiality. Above and beyond the question of whether or not pornography incites sex crimes is the more fundamental question never asked in Denmark: is engulfment by obscenity a wise thing in general? To a clinician, equating all expressions of sexuality, however vulgar and dehumanizing some of them are, making them available to the public without restriction, raising them to the level of a *sexual custom* or *institution,* is to loosen man's intellectual control over the sexual instincts. This is the violation of the universal social contract whereby men master instinctual drives by agreed-upon self-restraint to serve the best interests of the community in which they all reside.

Through the millennia, man has been constantly plagued

by the consequences of his failure to develop appropriate controls over the sexual instinct and at the same time provide for gratifying it. Advocacy of the misuse of sex, the demeaning of sex, the insult to mind, body, and human relationships leveled by pornography—all these exacerbate the difficulties of successfully living with our instincts.

The Danes, however, feel that pornography can be used even as a medium of sex education. The so-called "sex education" afforded by pornography has nothing to do with reality, nor is that its purpose. Pornography is harmful because inevitably it distorts sex by exaggeration or by combining it with violence, hate, and sadism. The purpose of education is to educate a child to *reality*, not to fantasy.

The contention that pornography acts as a safety valve for those suffering from perversions, such as voyeurism, fetishism, sadomasochism, and homosexuality, has no validity either. In my two decades of experience in treating serious sexual disorders I have found that those deeply troubled by such disturbances cannot find an outlet for the powerful emotions which demand release except in directly experiencing the perverse act itself. This behavior, unconsciously determined, is commonly antisocial, invades the rights of others, and must be compulsively repeated. The loss of self-esteem, the guilt, and the anxiety of those so afflicted are immense. The only genuine and enduring relief is through intensive psychoanalytic therapy. Pornography offers only an opportunity for encouraging already sick fantasies.

A man overwhelmed by voyeuristic impulses cannot be satisfied and quieted by viewing a nude woman in a magazine or on stage. In the consultation room he reveals his urge actually to *invade* the other's privacy without the other's knowledge, feeling that his victims are at his disposal, under his control; thus he gains a feeling of possessing the power and masculinity which otherwise he feels he lacks.

The decompensated voyeur, one for whom the perverse act no longer seems to reduce severe anxieties, undergoes a transformation wherein the obligatory act of observing a woman in a state of undress, in sexual intercourse, or while carrying out various bodily functions turns into an irresistible desire first to touch, then to grab—next to rape—and, finally, to destroy. For him pornography cannot substitute for real personal victimization. Thus, there is an intimate connection between voyeurism, sexual sadism, and sex crimes. Pornography *gratifies* none of these perversions, although it may help inspire variational expressions on the central theme with which they are unconsciously concerned.

The Parliament of Great Britain in the late 1960s urged the repeal of most laws against pornography—all except those which "protect" children and prohibit offensive public display. But one cannot have it both ways: legal but not on display. Legalization permits sale and, as with any merchandise, profitable transactions depend upon visibility. Visibility results in proliferation.

A case in point is that of the first "sex fair" in history, which took place in Copenhagen in 1968 and has resulted in "branch fairs" elsewhere, including an ocean-going fair aboard a large steamship traveling to major ports around the world. This fair is also an example of the impossibility of enforcing limits. Scandinavia promulgated its freedom by assurances that pornography would not be flagrantly on display. Nonetheless, a movie of the Copenhagen sex fair, in the guise of a "documentary," has been shown in the United States, and its in-person performers are on view wherever an audience congregates.

The Parliamentary committee found that very few people have been corrupted by an "obscene work." This suggests that "no one was ever raped by a book," or is tantamount to saying "no one is ever influenced by a film or a picture"—a patently false conclusion. Reading and viewing pave the way to action, for thinking is trial action.

If pornography is allowed to become culturally normative and legally valid, it will unquestionably affect not only many individuals in terms of their conceptualization of sexuality, but will also influence our national standards and sexual codes.

A telling example of the effect of a pornographic theme was recounted to me by a patient. Before undergoing psychoanalytic treatment, he had been convicted on a charge of peeping (voyeurism) and attempted rape. He spent nine years in prison, during which time he continually read and re-read a novel in which the protagonist holds a girl captive, helpless, completely in his power, and at the mercy of his taunts, sexual threats, and abuse.

From the first reading, my patient was obsessed by this story and waited only for the day when, upon his release, he would be able to act it out. Far from satisfying his perversion, pornography fed it. One might argue that the man was peculiarly susceptible because of his sexual pathology. But who knows how many other troubled persons, whose impulses (fortunately for society) remain dormant through the strength of suppression and/or repression, are precipitated into action through the impact of the printed page, television screen, or movies?

The proof of pornography's power has been the very popularity of such books, both as best sellers and films. They appeal to vast audiences precisely because of their theme: man's aggressive "power play," arising from unresolved infantile feelings of sexual inadequacy to a desire for complete control of "love objects." Pornography touches upon the universal conflict of infantile inadequacy and the illusion of infantile omnipotence—we were once all helpless children who believed our will dominated everyone around us. Many of us have never fully outgrown this stage, which is natural enough in infancy. The result is the wish to force others to "love us" even if it causes them suffering or costs them their lives. To my patient such a book provided active encouragement to his murderous, hostile sexual impulses.

Why are we unable to thwart the assault of pornography? Perhaps in part we suffer from a reaction to our former sexual puritanism, no longer a major force in this age of "sexual revolution." But the opposite extreme is not acceptable either. Our former reasons for objecting to pornography (i.e., false moralizing, fear of sexual stimulation) no longer have any force. We are confused by pornography because few are able to define it. We now know its central criteria, its cardinal traits—contaminated sex.

A second reason for our toleration is that as human beings we are all sexual creatures. Pornography writers exploit for commercial gain our conscious and unconscious reactions, reactions stemming from a normal function. Because we all have sexual instincts, we are all moved toward sources of sexual stimulation and arousal, for we find them pleasant and pleasurable. Only massive repression can completely eliminate the sex drive from consciousness.

Inasmuch as we are all sexual beings—that is, motivated by the desire for sexual pleasure—we may respond with some interest to the pornographic purveyor's work for the moment, until we are bored by its stereotypes, disgusted by its descriptions, horrified by its violence, sickened by its near-murderous aggression against the human spirit. We become muddled in our thinking as to the pernicious effect pornography has in general because most of us may initially feel some slight interest and, perhaps, even arousal to any or all sexual material, including that which borders on the pornographic or is unmistakably obscene. We should realize and accept our humanness but not become befogged by it—weaknesses, vulnerabilities, even sicknesses, exist; but they are not the *whole* story in human nature, and they shouldn't have the only voice in deciding social and personal issues.

A comparison to the aggressive instinct may prove helpful. In all of us there are fleeting or periodic feelings of rage which, in some instances, achieve the volume and intensity of a murderous impulse. A murderous fantasy may reach consciousness but must in time be put aside, suppressed, assimilated, or best of all, resolved by facing and conquering the fear which originally produced it. To foster that fear, persist in it, weave fantasies about it, embellish it, with readings about violence, to fan the fires of aggression with visualizations and portrayals of murder, arson, bombings, stabbings, is only to promote its possible future enactment. We all know we must reduce and control aggression to preserve ourselves and our society, and we must do the same with the pornography which celebrates our aggression.

Pornography cannot, of course, produce a sexual perversion in an adult without the etiological conflict of childhood. The nuclear conflicts leading to obligatory perversions and/ or severe sexual disorders come from the earliest years of life, sometimes before the child can read. But pornography can contribute to later complications and elaborations of serious sexual disturbance. It plays a large part in the *patterning* of the abnormal sexual behavior. Pornography is used by those suffering from perversions to help sustain the enactment of the perversion; it does not in any way alleviate the pressing emotional derangement of instinct and conflict, and is therefore valueless to those so unhappily afflicted.

Pornography does nothing to enrich our lives. It is one of those elements in our current era of sexual change which should be abolished, certainly not sanctioned by law. The only ones to profit from pornography are its purveyors. Pornography is now a billion-dollar business; it is safer than dope and more profitable than prostitution.

The findings of the President's Commission on Obscenity and Pornography[173] (I presented a rebuttal to the Commission's report before the subcommittee on postal operations of the House of Representatives in November of 1970[158]) may ultimately result in our laws being revised as they have been in Denmark. The Commission was in existence for two years, spent nearly two million dollars, and was comprised of eighteen members, only two of whom are psychiatrists. They recommended that all Federal, state, and local laws against pornography be repealed, with the proviso that children be protected from such material, not because it is potentially harmful to them, but because the parents *unjustifiably fear harm to them.*

The Commission states: "There are no recorded instances of sexual aggression, homosexuality, lesbianism, exhibitionism, or sexual abuse of children attributable to reading or viewing erotic stimuli among the several hundred participants in the twelve experiments reviewed."[173]

In our haste toward sexual freedom we are making a disastrous blunder, the enormity of which may perhaps not be known for many years. Making pornography a part of our cultural heritage, part of our institution of human courtship and mating, cannot fail to affect our youth and children, no matter what legal injunctions are placed against the young seeing a description on the printed page or depiction in film. The attitudes, ethics, and behavior of adults will be transmitted to succeeding generations simply by propinquity.

### *"The Peter Meter"*

Experiments were carried out by the Commission at the University of North Carolina in which instruments were used to measure the physical responses of twenty-three college men to prolonged exposure to erotic material.[173] The instrument apparently was a device to measure the size of the flaccid and erect penis—what I call the famous "peter meter." (I first became acquainted with the fact that the "peter meter" actually existed in 1969, when I had to comment unfavorably on a grant request for funds to support a transsexual-surgery project at a major Canadian medical center. Responses to individuals were to be judged by the volume changes recorded on the "peter meter" in an attempt to "scientifically objectify" what could have been ascertained by simple observation.)

The Commission's two major findings were that pornography does not cause sex crimes or corrupt minors. To dismiss the latter assertion, let me first point out that it is obvious that these "experiments" were not made on minors; the conclusion that minors below sixteen to eighteen are not affected is thus automatically invalid.

Basically the experiments performed by the Commission are worthless. At best they might identify some individuals already suffering from perversion, but this was not their intent. Their samples were not likely to include any such individuals in any case, as those so afflicted are not inclined to volunteer their services for fear of discovery. A male homosexual in such an experiment is apt to respond erotically to a picture of a nude male. On the other hand, I can state from twenty years of clinical experience that patients suffering from voyeurism will not respond erotically to pictures of nude females. Voyeurs, as earlier explained, require specific conditions for sexual arousal. They must be outside, in the dark, and peering *uninvited* into the woman's room. The Commission could hardly duplicate these conditions. Conditions encouraging sadistic behavior are still more difficult to reproduce in laboratories, for obvious reasons.

The knowledge that all of us can be sexually excited to some degree by depictions of erotic activity tends to blind would-be observers to both the quantitative and qualitative differences between those who have a normal response to what is erotic and maybe even pornographic, and those who have a pathological response. Certainly they lack completely the professional psychoanalytic training to enable them to discern each test subject's motivational state. To this shortcoming add the absence of individual clinical examinations in depth on a systematic basis. It is the motivational state of a person, not alone the concretion of his action, which reveals his true responses in any situation, and it is never more revealing than in determining the complicated emotions characteristic of sexual feelings.

That the would-be observers were handicapped from the start and could not carry out their job is plain. As I see it, the real goal of our society is to allow more access to sources of sexual gratification which are basically *healthy,* and to bar from approval and public dissemination all destructive insults to sex, to the body, to human relationships, and to the human spirit.

The crux of the censorship question should revolve around a distinction between pornographic material and erotic realism. The former distorts the realities upon which sexual maturity depends. Full and passionate sexuality is intensely rewarding. But this healthy sexuality cannot embrace any desire for violence, incest, sadism or other acts extinguishing human dignity.

# Chapter 7

# HOMOSEXUALITY

## A PERSONAL NARRATIVE

My clinical concern for the homosexual began in 1948 as a student at the Columbia University Psychoanalytic Clinic for Training and Research. In those days homosexuals were rarely accepted as patients; they were considered "too difficult" and the prognosis too uncertain. Little information about this condition was available. Many analysts were unwilling to take on homosexual patients because it was generally believed futile to treat anyone who appeared to be "satisfied" with his condition.

If little was known then about the male homosexual, even less was known about the female. Several senior analysts informed me that they had each seen only one or two female homosexual patients in their entire practice, and only for short periods of time. Except for the work of Helene Deutsch,[33, 34, 35] Marjorie Brierley,[20] and Ernest Jones[76] (the latter two in England), a few case reports by Sandor Lorand[101] and Gustav Bychowski,[23] plus other scattered data in the literature, material was virtually nonexistent. There were only two monographs on homosexuality, one in German, the other in French. The first was by Hans Sachs, "On the Genesis of Sexual Perversions"[136] (1923); the other,

"Homosexual Fixations in Neurotic Women"[138] (1929), by Raymond de Saussure.

The scattered bits and fragments of information I could track down were not sufficiently organized to be meaningful. How could it be, I wondered, that a widespread emotional disorder of such striking dimensions—a symptom picture which involved such a radical change in human relationships—had not undergone the most rigorous psychoanalytic investigation on a systematized basis?

My own first few homosexual patients semed to respond well to the psychoanalytic method, and I began to compile what scientific material there was on both male and female homosexuality.

In 1959, at my suggestion, the American Psychoanalytic Association conducted its first panel on the theoretical and clinical aspects of overt male homosexuality. My report of the panelists' deliberation was published in 1960.[146] The research activities it required were surpassed only by those for a second panel on the overt female homosexual two years later.[147] These explorations impelled me to pursue further the problem of homosexuality: its origins, unconscious mechanisms, and most efficacious therapy.

As a young analyst I had been perplexed by the uncertainties of causation, treatment, and outcome described in the limited literature then available. As my practice expanded, I observed common patterns in homosexuals, however apparently different from each other in family background, personal endowment, and current life-setting. Similar behavioral manifestations were apparent, and I began to formulate an etiology, developmental theory, and treatment approaches which proved effective in helping homosexual patients attain the goals they set for themselves before and during the course of therapy. Fifteen years of practice, teaching, and supervision of psychiatric residents, with continual refinement at the theoretical level, led me to the conclusions discussed in my book, *The Overt Homosexual* (1968). There is no question that by now we have sufficient evidence as a profession to demonstrate that homosexuality can be reversed in many cases or, at least, its symptoms and suffering greatly alleviated by medical psychoanalysis.

It was not my intention at the outset to spend much of my professional life exclusively in the treatment of individuals with sexual disorders. My field has been and continues to be the entire gamut of emotional disorders in all their forms. As it happened, one of my first psychoanalytic patients after graduating from the Columbia University Psychoanalytic Clinic was a young man of twenty-three. While treating him I ran headlong into the legal injustices perpetrated against homosexuals. At one crucial point in therapy, my patient was arrested and jailed, his record on being booked at the police station was stamped "DEGENERATE." This label, affixed to his name for life, had, needless to say, a deleterious effect on his therapeutic progress. It was many months before I could help him restore his shattered self-confidence. This kind of punishment and humiliation benefits neither the individual nor society, and it became my aim to do my utmost to correct the inequities against the homosexual and to document homosexuality as a psychiatric condition which needed investigation, research, and medical personnel trained to help the individual and enlighten the community.

In response to legal and social persecution, homosexual groups began in the sixties not only to turn on their persecutors, but also to turn against their medical (psychiatric) protectors who offered help and hope. In 1964, the report of the New York Academy of Medicine's Committee on Public Health revealed that some "homosexuals have gone beyond the plane of defensiveness and now argue that their deviancy is a 'desirable, noble, preferable way of life.' " Spokesmen for homosexual groups argued that homosexuality is not an aberration; those so oriented are merely a different kind of people living an acceptable way of life, and for one thing, they claim that it is the perfect answer to the problem of a population explosion.[!] The Committee concluded that "Homosexuality is indeed an illness. The homosexual is an emotionally disturbed individual who has not acquired the normal capacity to develop satisfying hetero-sexual relationships."[172]

This was clearly a disturbing trend I then saw developing, with homosexuals banding together, not to demand help from the medical profession and public recognition of their condition, but to proclaim their "normality" and attack any opposition to this view. This, as always, constituted a vocal but very small minority of homosexuals compared to the large numbers of homosexuals who would like more help, not less. In October of 1964, the nation was stunned by the sudden resignation of Walter Jenkins, President Johnson's confidant and aide. Mr. Jenkins had been arrested for homo-sexuality in a public place (a "morals" charge). An October 16 editorial in *The New York Times* stated: "As for Mr. Jenkins and his family, there can be only compassion. Their misfortune is not an occasion to indulge in self-righteous moralizing. Just as alcoholism and drug addiction have come to be recognized as diseases, so such sexual perversion is increasingly understood as an emotional illness." James A. Wechsler of the *New York Post* (Oct. 19, 1964) felt that "the real questions concern the code which permits us to doom this forty-six-year-old father of six children without any thoughtful further exploration." He deplored "the taboos that place the subject beyond the realm of serious discus-sion." Homosexuality was finally becoming a wide-open issue.

I decided that the moment had come to act directly on behalf of the homosexual and anyone else suffering from a sexual disorder, with the idea of making help available on request. I wrote to Stanley F. Yolles, M.D., then Director of the National Institutes of Mental Health, asking to meet with him to discuss some suggestions for a national program for the prevention and treatment of homosexuality and other sexual disorders. I wrote: "Of the whole range of sexual dis-orders, homosexuality is the most misunderstood. . . . The deep aversion that is aroused by this disorder is illustrated by public attitudes manifested toward it. . . . Homosexuality not only causes suffering for the individual resulting in grave loss to our national community, but is inimical to the preservation of the family unit. The pain and anguish of the homosexual himself, added to the damage to his family and close associates, produces tragic consequences. Modern medicine must (1) dispel the mystery which surrounds homosexuality; (2) dissolve the fear which attends any attempt at free discussion; (3) defeat the ubiquitous propaganda unfortunately used as a face-saving device by homosexual organizations to represent this condition as a 'way of life' rather than as a form of emotional illness or sexual immaturity."

Dr. Yolles encouragingly replied by suggesting that I meet with members of his staff to discuss methodologies, agency roles, and other factors that would be required to implement the programs I proposed. On February 3, 1965, I met at the National Institutes of Mental Health in Maryland with Eli A. Rubenstein, Ph.D., of the Training and Manpower Resources Branch, Harold M. Hildreth, M.D., James W. Osberg, M.D., and William G. Hollister, M.D., to propose the establishment of a Federal Medical Center for Sexual Rehabilitation. This presentation comprised plans for a complete project: location, building, equipment, staff, procedures, regional offices, public-health informational services, job descriptions, and organizational chart together with a detailed explanation of treatment procedures from voluntary admission through discharge. The federal government decided it could not or would not involve itself with homosexuality.

A project requiring years of planning and conceptualization was dismissed out of hand by representatives of our nation's central mental health service (NIMH), responsible for preserving and improving the mental health of the citizens of the most powerful nation in the world, for a condition estimated then to involve over five million adults. I went on writing and publishing my findings; subsequently, on the basis of these efforts, I was invited to address the Adult

Psychiatry Branch of the NIMH on the problem and treatment of homosexuality, this time participating in a lecture series sponsored by that institute.

Shortly thereafter the Director of the NIMH appointed a Task Force on Homosexuality. Two years later on October 10, 1969, the NIMH Task Force made its final report in which it acknowledged, at least in part, the validity of my earlier proposal by recommending "the coordination of NIMH activities in the broad area of sexual behavior by the establishment of a center for the study of sexual behavior."[119] This Task Force did not by any means represent the forefront of knowledge on the issue of homosexuality. Only three psychiatrists were participants. One of them, Dr. Judd Marmor, had for years espoused the view that homosexuality is normal. The chairman, a psychologist, Evelyn Hooker, Ph.D., was of the same long-time conviction. The Kinsey-Hopkins faction was represented by Paul Gebhardt, Ph.D., Director of the Institute for Sex, Indiana University, and John Money, Ph.D., from Johns Hopkins, a prime mover among the proponents for transsexual surgery. The law was represented by the Honorable David L. Bazelon, who at one point during the Task Force deliberations resigned. Bazelon, a professor of law, was also a member of the Social Science Research Council, a professor of sociology, and a vice-president of the Russell Sage Foundation. Psychoanalytic clinicians, such as Bieber,[14] myself, and others who had worked for many years in depth therapy with homosexual patients were pointedly left off this committe. On a subsequent occasion, I was told, by Paul Gebhardt that this action was taken as both Bieber and I were considered "professionally biased" because of our "Freudian" approach.

The NIMH report concluded: "Some of the primary goals of the NIMH center study of sexual behavior should be to develop knowledge, generate and disseminate information, mollify taboos and myths, provide rational basis for intervention, and provide data to policy makers for use in their efforts to frame rational social policy."[119] This report then proceeded to ask for society's toleration and understanding of the homosexual condition and the gradual removal of persecutory laws against such activities between consenting adults. These positions are good and well-taken. But where the report failed abysmally was that it never came to a direct conclusion as to whether exclusive homosexuality is a form of emotional illness, of arrested psychosexual development, or a pathological condition.

Meanwhile militant homosexual groups continued to attack any psychiatrist or psychoanalyst who dared to present his findings as to the psychopathology of homosexuality before national or local meetings of psychiatrists or in public forums. For example, while the NIMH Task Force was deliberating in June of 1968, I addressed the annual convention of the American Medical Association on "Homosexuality and Medicine." My comments appeared on the front page of the *San Francisco Chronicle*. The next day, at the insistence of the homosexual societies that they be given "equal time," a countering article appeared falsely accusing me of asking for "involuntary" and forced treatment of homosexuals. The publication of "Homosexuality and Medicine" in the *Journal of the American Medical Association*[157] in 1970, however, produced a deluge of supportive letters from all over the world, including Eastern European countries and small villages in Africa. Having presented the issue squarely before the largest medical affiliation in the world, I felt that the next most direct step should be taken in Manhattan, the mecca of homosexuality. I formed a group of colleagues with excellent qualifications in the treatment of sexual disorders and proposed to the New York County District Branch of the American Psychiatric Association that it be constituted as an official committee of that organization. Thus, the first all-psychiatric Task Force on Homosexuality was born. It has been the only such medically oriented body in the country.

After two years of deliberations and sixteen meetings, this Task Force, composed of a dozen experts affiliated with the major medical centers in New York City, submitted its report on homosexuality to the Executive Council of the

New York Country District Branch of the American Psychiatric Association. In essence it unanimously documented the fact that exclusive homosexuality was a disorder of psychosexual development, and simultaneously asked for civil rights for those suffering from the disorder. The report was "not acceptable" to the new members (and some old) of the Executive Committee. The message was coming through loud and clear: the only report acceptable would have been one which was not only in favor of civil rights but one which declared homosexuality *not* a psychosexual disorder; we reached this conclusion upon careful examination of their objections and their inconsistencies. The matter was discussed with Dr. Osnos of New York, the Executive Committee's representative, to no avail. The committee was then dissolved and the report buried. Its members, determined that it see the light of day, published it as a "study-group" report in late spring of 1974.[70]

In 1973 a movement first spearheaded by Vice President Marmor of the A.P.A. and other psychiatrists in league with the Gay Activists Alliance, the Mattachine Society, and the Daughters of Bilitis (the women's arm of the Mattachine Society), undertook to influence the Nomenclature Committee of the Association to delete "homosexuality" from the diagnostic nomenclature. Moving swiftly, a small band of well-intentioned but misguided psychiatrists, disregarding a large body of scientific evidence to the contrary, accomplished what every other society with rare exceptions (Ancient Greece for a short period during an adolescent's life, pre-Meiji Japan, certain top echelons of the Nazi party, and special status groups such as the berdaches, Nata slaves, and Chukchee shamans) would have trembled to attempt— the revision of a basic concept of life and biology: that men and women normally mate with the opposite, not the same, sex.

On December 14, 1973, the Board of Trustees meeting in Washington, D.C., officially declared homosexuality a normal form of sexual life and, in essence and by direct implication, of equal value for the individual and society.

Any disturbances of abnormality in the homosexual were henceforth to be attributed only to the homosexual's dissatisfaction that he is homosexual—as if he had simply bought a suit of clothes that he no longer liked and was being "neurotic" about it if he complained.

The consequences of this action are of a formidable nature. Not only will the homosexual be victimized, but the entire area of research in the development of gender-identity will be damaged. Young men and women with relatively minor sexual fears of the opposite sex will be led with equanimity by psychiatrists and other members of the medical profession who buy this bill of boods into a self-despising pattern and lifestyle. Homosexuality will henceforth be touted as simply an acceptable variation on the norm. Adolescents, nearly all of whom suffer from some sort of uncertainty as to identity, will be discouraged from assuming that one form of gender-identity (one's own birth-right) is preferable to another.[16] And those persons who already have a homosexual problem will be discouraged from fighting their way out of a self-destructive fantasy, discouraged from learning to accept themselves as male or female, discouraged from all of those often painful but necessary courses that allow us all to function as reasonable and participating individuals in a cooperating society.

Over the past twenty years homosexuality has come "out of the closet" scientifically.* Is the medical investigation of homosexuality now to be plunged once again into darkness by the disastrous declaration that it is a noncondition?

And what then of the fate of society? Abram Kardiner, former Professor of Psychiatry at Columbia University, recipient of the Humanities Prize of the *New York Times* in 1966, and expert in the area of psychoanalytic investigation of cultures, warns:

> There is an *epidemic* form of homosexuality, which is more than the usual incidence, which generally occurs in

---

* See references 14, 18, 36, 37, 107, 132, 135, 148, 149, 151, 152, 153, 155, 159, 162.

social crises or in declining cultures when license and
boundless permissiveness dulls the pain of ceaseless anxiety,
universal hostility and divisiveness. Thus in Betsileo the incidence of homosexuality was visibly increased at a time
when the society was in a state of collapse.

A powerful lobby of "gay" organizations has brought
pressure on the American Psychiatric Association to remove
homosexuality from the category of aberrancy. This is only
one facet of the tidal wave of egalitarianism and divisiveness that is sweeping the country. Even schizophrenia is
being promoted to the category of a *life style*. But this
egalitarianism is bound to exact a high price from the community . . . [for it is a] symptom of a social distress syndrome.

Supporting the claims of the homosexuals and regarding
homosexuality as a normal variant of sexual activity is to
deny the social significance of homosexuality. To do this is
to give support to the divisive elements in the community.
. . . Above all it militates against the family and destroys
the function of the latter as the last place in our society
where affectivity can still be cultivated.

Homosexuals cannot make a society, nor keep ours going
for very long. It operates against the cohesive elements in
society in the name of a fictitious freedom. It drives the opposite sex into a similar direction. And no society can long
endure when either the child is neglected or when the sexes
war upon each other.[84]


# THE MISCONCEPTIONS

## *The Public's Confusion*

In the last twenty years the nation has become enmeshed
in an ideological crisis over the issue of homosexuality. Its
resolution may ultimately be recorded as a decisive one in
American sexual mores and behavior. The situation is very
complex, much of it distorted and misunderstood. It is such
a specialized problem that few can remain objective about

it, yet the issue must be faced squarely; otherwise future generations will continue to encounter the same problem in greater intensity and complexity.

The increased visibility of homosexuality leaves its mark on those who are themselves homosexual or inclined in that direction, on our culture, our institutions, our creative and artistic patterns, and, especially, on family life—the basic unit of society. It has been suggested by the very small number of homosexuals organized into highly vocal groups who take the position that they speak for all homosexuals, that homosexuality should be encouraged.

Many of us feel detached, even unconcerned, about the issue of homosexuality. But unless we face the problem in its full dimensions, the matter may in time be taken out of the realm of medicine and left entirely to punitive legal measures for solution. This would relegate it to agencies not equipped to recognize and deal with the true meaning of this condition.

Part of the Gay Liberation movement's seeming attractiveness to some segments of the public is that it appears to be revolutionary; theirs is not, however, a new position. There have been comparable movements by homosexuals in the past, well documented by Arno Karlen in his book, *Sexuality and Homosexuality.*[85]

Homosexual revolutionists state that homosexuality should be granted total acceptance as a valid form of sexual functioning, different from but equal to heterosexuality. Such acceptance of homosexuality, as simply a variation of normality, is naïve, to say the least. Equally misleading is the idea that it is merely an aspect of normal development, a transient state of adolescence, without meaningful consequences. That we as a nation could be persuaded to overlook such tendencies among our young people is a harmful fantasy, yet prevalent, as shown by the fact that colleges can be pressured to charter homosexual groups on campus, with all the privileges of other scholastic and social organizations, thereby lending tacit approval. Homosexual "clubs" are

now going into our high schools as well. Even the legal age
for homosexual "consenting adults" has been lowered to
fourteen in Hawaii.

The implications of such trends are profound. They make
the adolescent uncertain and confused. Even for an adult,
struggling to strengthen what may be a frail heterosexual
orientation, the vicissitudes of maintaining sexual adequacy
may drive him into a homosexual pattern. He does not know
how else to resolve the deep conflicts which have persisted
and tortured him since early childhood. Homosexuality is
a foredoomed attempt to find a panacea for the tormenting
fear which originated in early childhood and, like any fantasy solution, remains unsatisfactory at all times and disastrous much of the time.

Some borderline individuals are misled into accepting
homosexual life as normal. Many homosexuals know that
this is a falsehood, but feel the existence of this propaganda
must have some basis in fact, simply because it's so widespread. They are left with the conviction that there is no
hope in attempting a reversal of their condition. We can only
speculate as to the number of hopeless people who may have
committed suicide, unhappy with their homosexuality and
believing it to be an irreversible condition.

The greatest damage from this propaganda is to the young,
adolescents and youths who are knocked off balance by an
upsurge of homosexual desire and interest and who know
of no way to deal with it. One of the far-reaching effects
of such propaganda is that these younger people who could
be helped so much more readily at an earlier age have to
undergo a period of intense bitterness and disillusionment
in discovering that they cannot possibly live a happy homosexual life. Influenced and deterred by unfortunate and unrealistic publicity, it is years before they seek medical help.

Another form of propaganda is the idea that since certain
highly creative individuals have been homosexuals, homosexuality is a sign of creativity or imaginative superiority.
Like everyone else, homosexuals have conflict-free areas of

the ego which, of course, allow for productive functioning; and if the individual is exceptionally gifted, achievement may be very high despite an underlying emotional problem.

As early as 1920, Freud noted with regard to homosexuals' claim to superiority that often, but not always, homosexuals "are men and women who otherwise have reached an irreproachably high standard of mental growth and development, intellectually and ethically, and are only afflicted with this one fateful peculiarity. Through the mouths of their . . . spokesman, they lay claim to being a special variety of the human race, a 'third sex,' as they call it, standing with equal rights alongside the other two. They are not, of course, as some might maintain, the elect of mankind; they contain in their ranks at least as many inferior and worthless individuals as can be found among those differently constituted sexually."[46]

The issue of homosexuality is dominated by emotional thinking which cannot help but generate confusion, fear, and rage. These charged attitudes have become widespread throughout the community, and compound the difficulties in dealing with what is really a major health problem. Polls have shown that the majority of the public still favors legal punishment for homosexual acts, even if performed in private; homosexuality is considered more harmful to society than adultery, and even than abortion. In our culture the very thought of effeminacy in the male—although homosexuality does not necessarily mean effeminacy—is tremendously disturbing.

The historical evidence of the practice of homosexuality from earliest recorded times has led to grave misconceptions. For example, homosexuals often feel that if this condition has existed over so many centuries, what hope is there of eliminating it? This defeatism is shared by the public and, unfortunately, influences our laws and our scientific objectivity. Rather than assume that homosexuality is an inevitable component of the human condition, it better behooves us to acknowledge that homosexuality is a form of psycho-

sexual immaturity which has not yet been adequately
studied by those who are best trained to investigate and
treat it.

The acceptance of homosexuality as a normal form of
sexual life is dangerous and disabling to the public welfare
and to the individuals directly concerned. The underlying
pain and anguish of the homosexual, if added to the damage
done to his family, produces consequences beyond the imagination of anyone not in a position to observe personally the
intensity of suffering. Many late-adolescent suicides, especially those at colleges, may be in fact due to severe pain and
anguish having to do with homosexuality. A recent survey
by the National Institutes of Mental Health has determined
that the majority of suicides during the early college years
were over the conflict of sexual identity. Over one-third of
Harvard-Radcliffe student suicide attempts (25 out of 69,
or 37%) between 1963 and 1967 were made by individuals
severely disturbed by homosexual conflicts.[21]

## Sources of Public Confusion

Professionals have done their share to confuse the issue.
A social psychiatrist, Martin Hoffman, has compiled statements gathered from homosexuals in bars, Turkish baths,
etc., and presented them in a book, *The Gay World*.[68] His
conclusions were derived from questionnaires and brief
non-analytic interviews in informal contexts. From this du-
bious material he erroneously concludes that homosexuality
is not a disorder but a "different" form of sexuality. His idea
is that homosexuals are not ill at all except for any chance
concomitant illness completely unrelated to their homosexuality. Data collected in this manner and in such settings
cannot be taken seriously, studded as they are with rationalizations and devoid of rigorous scientific methodology on
the part of the author.

Wainwright Churchill III, an American psychiatrist practicing in Rome, is the author of *Homosexual Behavior*

*Among Males: A Cross-Cultural and Cross-Species Investigation.* His observations, equally erroneous as Hoffman's and also derived partially in Turkish baths, lead him to state that "Exclusive homosexuality may often, though not necessarily always, be associated with fears of heterosexuality. . . . Even heterosexuality, according to most analysts [he includes Freud in this group by quoting him out of context], is the result of the repression and sublimation of homosexual trends, while exclusive homosexuality is the result of the repression of heterosexual trends."[!] After this rather pat and Alice-in-Wonderlandish conclusion, Churchill continues, "ambisexuality, rather than exclusive sexuality of any kind, is the biological norm [and] comes from large scale statistical studies of sexual behavior in our society—cross-cultural investigation and cross-species investigation."[25]

This conclusion has long been refuted. For example, Gadpaille, a psychiatrist who has worked extensively on the social aspects of homosexuality, points out that "the use of culture as a definitional basis for species normality is on very shaky anthropological footing; cross-cultural data readily yield endless examples of culturally sanctioned behavior which could only be considered pathological. . . ."[51]

It is necessary to realize that the comments of both Hoffman and Churchill are derived from nonpsychoanalytic material. The mildest criticism one can make regarding these investigators is that they describe events at the most superficial level. To accept such superficiality would be to set back scientific understanding to the pre-Freudian period, before the complex mechanisms of denial and rationalization were thoroughly understood.

But the duped and misinformed, unfortunately, are found in many high places. Mrs. Rita E. Hauser, United States representative to the United Nations Human Rights Commission, stated in St. Louis on August 10, 1970 (as reported in *The New York Times*), that laws banning marriage between persons of the same sex were unconstitutional. Speaking on "Women's Liberation and the Constitution" at a meeting of the American Bar Association, Mrs. Hauser said that such laws were based on what she called an outdated notion that reproduction is the purpose of marriage. She argued that overpopulation has made this rationale obsolete. "Limited reproduction has now become the social goal . . . and I know no better way of accomplishing this than marriage between the same sexes." There are many ways of limiting reproduction other than endorsing marriage between members of the same sex; a chemical is far better.

## The Reality of Homosexuality

Above all, the homosexual must be recognized as an individual who suffers from a psychiatric problem.

Only in the consultation room does the homosexual truly reveal himself and his worlds, both inner and outer. No other data, statistics, or statements can be accepted as setting forth the true nature of homosexuality. All other sources must necessarily be heavily weighted by face-saving devices or rationalizations or, if they issue from lay persons, lack of scientific and medical background on which to base and support their views. The best thing that can be said for the well-intentioned but unqualified observer is that he is misguided because he cannot apply those techniques which would make it possible to discern the deeply underlying clinical picture. He cannot evaluate the emotional patterns and interpersonal events in the life of a homosexual.

Some homosexuals bridle at being considered as having emotional problems. Having had no hope for years, they see no help for their condition. Their symptom is "ego syntonic," that is, it provides a partial equilibrium to an otherwise recurrently intolerable anxiety state. Most homosexuals are not aware that their sexual acts help to relieve the inner pressures of their deep conflicts; often they cannot understand that a person may be deeply troubled and not realize it. The proof of this assertion is demonstrated by the fact that any attempt to cease homosexual activities produces intense anxiety, tension, and depression.

I am often asked to explain why heterosexuality is "normal." One way of answering this is to ask what is pathology (nonnormality)? Pathology, organically and physiologically, is defined as a failure to function usually coexisting with pain and/or suffering. The same failure of functioning can be applied to psychological conditions. It is this failure and its manifold meanings which are so obvious in obligatory homosexuality. Beneath the obvious failure of the male-female functional design lies the multiple searing, agonizing sorrows, tragedies, fears, and guilts of both an unconscious and conscious nature which pervade the homosexual's life. Some therapists who do not practice in-depth psychotherapy do not know or tend to overlook these basic facts.

Early unconscious fears are responsible for the later development of homosexuality and other modified sexual patterns of the obligatory type. They have in common the inability to perform in a standard male-female design and, as one of their aims, the achievement or orgastic release. If an individual engages in sexual contact with persons of the same sex repeatedly and out of inner necessity (compulsion) and, if when he forces himself to function in any other way, he does so (if at all) with very little or no pleasure, he may be considered to be an obligatory homosexual. But we must remember that he behaves this way out of inner necessity. *He has no choice*, the decision having been made by his unconscious.

We believe today that homosexuality should be classified in the following way. There are two major types of homosexuality within a motivational schema: obligatory (true) homosexuality and episodic homosexual *behavior*.

Obligatory homosexuality is reparative in nature and is ushered in by the inhibition of standard sexual performance through early fears. It arises from processes of psychological repair (analogous to processes of physiological repair after direct bodily injury), which in the main are unconscious and are marked by a high degree of inflexibility. Usually, obligatory homosexual acts are frequent. Some individuals, however, struggle mightily to resist their impulses so that they may appear to be of the episodic type in terms of incidence.

In true episodic homosexual behavior, homosexual acts are the result of conscious deliberation rather than an unconscious compulsion and, as a rule, are dropped as soon as the situation changes.

Situational or episodic homosexuality occurs where the lack of opportunity for heterosexual contact may push an individual to seek homosexual orgastic outlet. Such a situation may occur in institutions which enforce segregation of the sexes, such as the prison community.

Too often, the average person either fears the homosexual or laughs at him, wishes to punish him or avoids him. These attitudes are similar to those formerly directed toward the "spastic" or neurologically deformed, and promote the homosexual's tendency to isolation and the formation of groups whose aim is largely to foster homosexuality as a special way of life (this latter move is implemented by only a relatively small number of homosexuals). Unfortunately, by retaining legal sanctions against him, the public justifies the homosexual's uniting with other homosexuals as a "minority" group. By punishing him with prison or fines, the public proclaims that the homosexual is "bad," guilty, and a criminal.

How can the homosexual accept the reality of his condition and do something about it, if he is not even informed of its nature by medical science; if he is not protected by laws and the culture as a whole by being granted all his civil rights?

Homosexuality is unique as a defense mechanism. It has the capacity to neutralize profound psychic conflicts, temporarily producing pseudo-equilibrium and a pleasure reward (orgasm). It thereby permits the individual to function. This neutralization of conflict allows for the growth of certain ego-adaptive elements of the personality; thus, the homosexual may, for long intervals, give the impression that he is completely happy.

He himself often asks if there is not some kind of genetic[79] or hormonal factor,[66] innate or inborn, which accounts for his condition. Homosexuality is not innate. There is no connection between sexual instinct and the selection of sexual object,[42, 124] nor can any chemical imbalance determine the kind of partner preferred for sexual intercourse. Such selection is learned, acquired behavior; there is no inevitable genetic or hormonal inborn propensity toward a partner of either the same or opposite sex. However, the *male-female design*[124] is exemplified to the child from birth and culturally ingrained through the marital order. This design is anatomically determined, as it derives from cells which in the evolutionary scale underwent changes into organ systems and finally into individuals reciprocally adapted to each other. This is the evolutionary development of man. The male-female design is thus perpetually maintained, and only overwhelming fear can disturb or divert it.

A biological argument has been attributed to Ford and Beach (1951) in connection with their research on infrahuman species such as cattle, dogs, and primates. It is claimed that same-sex mounting behavior is evidence of inborn homosexual patterns which can be generalized to humans. One of the world's leading experts on animal behavior, Beach corrected this erroneous interpretation in 1971: "I don't know any authenticated instance of males or females in the animal world preferring a homosexual partner—if by homosexual you mean complete sexual relations, including climax—it's questionable that mounting in itself can properly be called sexual" (Karlen, 1971).

Homosexuals often express doubt about whether their condition can ever be reversed. The homosexual who attempts to extricate himself from a community of homosexuals is tagged a "traitor," one who threatens to invalidate their claims of "having been born that way," of being "special." It is not uncommon for homosexuals to warn any individual attempting treatment that change would, at best, prove only superficial.

Fear of incurability as well as of treason are part of the

problem. A homosexual himself reported to me during the course of psychoanalysis,

> I've just got to get this homosexual monkey off my back. I just frankly can't live with it. I must either extinguish it, if I can, or maybe by religion extinguish all sex. And the other thing is to be dead. To have anonymous sex with other sick men, I can't make a life out of that. . . . The homosexuals I know think I am copping out, and if it's not hereditary they feel at least it's chemical and impossible to change. They say to me, "Once homosexuality is established, you can't get out, or if you do try to get out you'll go nuts." They tell you that you will be isolated and they keep telling you you're a traitor trying to leave the group, turning against your own kind, you are trying to do something and be something that you're not. They say you're self-indulgent and selfish, feeding your ego in a very selfish kind of way, and that you're enjoying your neurosis in trying to get well. . . . Homosexuals are destructive people, even in the actual sexual act, and homosexuality is only progressive moral, emotional, and physical deterioration.

A stronger and more desperate cry for help would be difficult to imagine.

### Homosexual vs. Heterosexual Love Relationships

The question is often asked, Is there any difference between heterosexual and homosexual love relationships? The answer is, most emphatically, yes. In heterosexuality, the masculine needs of the male become to a great extent "ego-invested." The ego feels the need to discharge personally and directly this masculine tension. His feminine needs become "object-invested," which means that the ego feels the need for a female sexual partner whose feminine urges it cares to satisfy. In offering this satisfaction, his ego obtains vicarious gratification of its own feminine needs. The more the male ego "egotizes" the urges of its own sex and externalizes to an appropriate object-representation the urges of the opposite sex, the more does the ego feel complete.

On the other hand, the more his ego "egotizes" the biological urges of the opposite sex, for the satisfaction of which it is not anatomically and physiologically equipped, and externalizes the urges of its own sex onto an object-representation, the more it feels mutilated. This important contribution to the understanding of human sexuality was made by the late Eduardo Weiss,[180] a prominent Chicago analyst and friend of Freud.

Dr. Weiss thus explained one of the basic mechanisms involved in the choice of a particular lover. A man is attracted to and falls in love with that particular woman who represents his own feminine needs and desires and enjoys her femininity vicariously. A woman will love a particular man because of the very masculine qualities which are a projection of her own masculine needs and drives, and which she then can enjoy vicariously. Thus the love relationship between male and female produces the feeling of being whole and complete and then of transcending the two individual selves in a union which possesses an intrinsic strength of its own: the eternal secret of sexual attraction between man and woman.

The homosexual is engaged in an ego-saving operation to compensate for the defect in his masculinity; he therefore seeks out the masculinity in another man which he then can incorporate. Such compensation via incorporation is fleeting in its fulfilling effect; it requires continuous repetition, as this stolen masculinity is not genuine and is doomed to failure. It must constantly be replenished in order for the individual to feel strengthened by it. It is apparent therefore that "homosexual love" springs from totally different motivations then does heterosexual love.

## Cultural Studies

Homosexuality, present throughout the ages, can be found in almost all cultures. It has been treated in ways ranging from tolerance to hostile rejection. Efforts to deal with it can be traced to some of the earliest writings—for example, the laws of Hammurabi (second century B.C.) in Babylon, to Egyptian papyri in which it is referred to as an ancient custom of the gods, to the Old Testament, where it is described as a "sin and scourge," e.g., Sodom and Gomorrah. Under Roman law many aspects of homosexuality were ignored, especially female homosexuality. Early Anglo-Saxon laws were not as lenient but it has been inaccurate to regard taboos against homosexuality as deriving entirely from the Judeo-Christian code. During the Dark Ages, homosexuality was regarded as a form of heresy, and those "afflicted" were burnt at the stake.

Contrary to popular opinion, the practice of homosexuality in ancient Greece was merely situational and variational, the latter being motivated by the desire for "extra" thrills. It is now clear that Greece, during the Hellenistic period, invoked severe penalties and enacted strict laws against homosexual activities. W. K. Lacey, of Cambridge University, writes in his volume *The Family in Classical Greece,* as follows: "We are sometimes told that the Greeks were fully bisexual, enjoying both homosexual and heterosexual intercourse, and that romantic love in Greece was associated with attachments to boys and not to girls. Whatever the truth of the latter statement, there can be no doubt that, while the Greeks had a deep admiration for the physical beauty of the young male, in Athens the practice of sodomy was strictly circumscribed by the law."[94]

Boys still at school were protected against sexual assaults by a law (said to go as far back as Draco and Solon, seventh and sixth centuries B.C.). Adult citizens (those enrolled on the demoregisters) who were catamites (those engaging in anal intercourse) or had been catamites as adults, suffered a diminution of civic rights; those who procured free boys for sodomy are said to have been punishable by law. Sodomy was thought reprehensible for older men even when the catamite was not a citizen, as is clear from a speech of Lysias, but it was not illegal; it may be that the law in this field was similar to that for adultery—what was quite legal with slaves and other noncitizens was illegal with citizens, and the law took notice of the private morals of individuals, and punished offenders.

"Pederasty was expensive," Lacey continues. "Whether this was because the youths' admirers wanted to compete in generosity for favours or the youths were able to use the law virtually to blackmail their admirers no doubt varied in individual cases. Plato's attack on sodomy, especially in the *Laws*, reveals that the practice was not unknown to him, and that it was more repugnant to his ideals than heterosexual intercourse outside marriage, since this latter (if secret) was tolerated in the *Laws* as a second-best to the ideal of virginity till marriage and sexual intercourse only within marriage for the purpose of breeding children."[94]

In the Homeric period, the absence of pederasty coincided with the more elevated status of women, whereas in the historic period, the presence of pederasty coincided with degraded status of women.

Variational forms of episodic homosexuality may occur in individuals who yield to the desire for an alteration of sexual excitement. In some cultures, such surplus activity is a part of the established social order; in others, it is entirely a matter of individual enterprise. An institutional form of episodic homosexuality occurs in certain tribes as part of the customs of their particular culture.[81] These were rites or symbolic activities of the cultural unit. The motivations behind variational forms of episodic homosexual behavior are as varied as the motivations which drive men and women to seek power, gain protection, assure dependency, seek security, wreak vengeance, or experience specialized sensations. The choices, however are *consciously* made, deliberate, and usually given up when the situation has improved for the individual. If they are not given up it is because there is personal gain of an economic or social nature.

Kardiner, in a psychoanalytic-anthropological study, has shown that in the Comanche tribes of the midwestern United States there was no homosexuality; an occasional transvestite was treated like a foolish old woman. It was completely un-adaptive for a young man to be homosexual in the Comanche tribe, as the tribe was geared for warfare and for hunting. All children were bound physically close to the mother for the first year or two of life. Boys were thereafter turned over to the father and the other men (the mother freely relin-quishing any emotional control over her son) to begin train-ing and cultivation of those attributes and skills leading to being successful warriors and hunters.[81]

Observers of kibbutz-reared children in Israel have re-ported that there was no evidence of homosexuality in adult-hood, indicating that in a fairly conservative and highly structured communal-nursery situation, appropriate gender-identification is encouraged. The Israeli situation is one in which pressing national conditions (a permanent state of war-alert and a severe manpower problem) have necessi-tated communal child-raising. This situation, however, has *not* meant a relaxation of old principles of child-rearing, but rather a strengthening of them.

## The "New" Venereal Disease

The current increase in homosexuality causes other social problems than those mentioned above. There are reports that gonorrhea is getting tougher than ever to cure. It is well known that the spread of venereal disease is highest among homosexuals, with their tremendous number of transient sexual contacts. Gonorrhea organisms are increasingly drug-resistant. Dr. McKinsey Pollock, a public-health specialist, states that we are getting to the "physical upper limit of treatment that can be given at one time, and we have to give it at one time to get high blood levels." (*Medical World News,* August 8, 1969.) It must also be remembered that there is a tendency for homosexuals to engage in group sex with multiple contacts. In Manhattan, for example, there are several bars where hundreds of homosexuals gather in a back room for orgiastic activity. Two or three partners may be simultaneously performing—one engaging in fellatio, the other in anal intercourse on the same individual. Men are lined up, one behind the other, to suck the penis of a particular man. In the course of ten or eleven hours, a homosexual population of two or three hundred within such a single back room will produce in geometric progression a tremendous number of gonorrheal and syphilitic infections.

A third and "new" venereal disease is infectious hepatitis of the non-serum type. Because homosexual practices often involve analingus and anal intercourse, one person suffering from infectious hepatitis may pass the organism through his feces and infect multiple scores of individuals.

## Two Dramatists Look at Homosexuality

The following dialogue, excerpted from a recent play by the eminent Tennessee Williams (playwright) is spoken by a character identified as Young Man:

> There's a coarseness, a deadening coarseness, in the experience of most homosexuals. The experiences are quick, and hard, and brutal, and the pattern of them is practically unchanging. Their act of love is like the jabbing of a hypodermic needle to which they're addicted but which is more and more empty of real interest and surprise.
>
> Whenever I would feel this—*feeling*, this—shock of—what?—self-realization?—I would be stunned, I would be thunderstruck by it. And by the existence of everything that exists, I'd be lightening struck with astonishment. . . .
>
> It would do more than astound me, it would give me a feeling of panic, the sudden sense of—I suppose it was like an epileptic seizure, except that I didn't fall to the ground in convulsions; no, I'd be more apt to try to lose myself in a crowd on a street until the seizure was finished. They were dangerous seizures.
>
> One time I drove into the mountains or smashed the car into a tree, and I'm not sure I *meant* to do that, or . . . in a forest you'll sometimes see a giant tree, several hundred

years old, that's scarred, that's blazed by lightening, and the world is most obscured by the obstinately still living and growing bark. I wonder if such a tree has learned the same lesson that I have, not to feel astonishment any more but just go on, continue for two or three hundred years more?

This boy I picked up tonight, the kid from the tall corn country, still has the capacity for being surprised by what he sees, hears and feels in this kingdom of earth. All the way up the canyon to my place, he kept saying, *I can't believe it, I'm here, I've come to the Pacific, the world's greatest ocean!*—as if nobody, Magellan or Balboa or even the Indians, had ever seen it before him; yes, like he'd discovered this ocean, the largest on earth, and so now, because he'd found it himself, it existed, now, for the first time, never before . . . And this excitement of his reminded me of my having lost the ability to say: "My God!" instead of just: "Oh, well."[182]

The best example of responsible creative writing about homosexuality was achieved in a play which arrived on Broadway in 1969. This drama, *The Boys in the Band*,[30] is a searing exposition of the homosexual condition. It affords insight into the personal anguish, the apathy, the discomforts, the unhappiness involved in this masquerade of life. It makes one sympathetic to the homosexual and dispels the abhorrence which many individuals feel toward him. It is this kind of presentation which will lead to changes in the law as we rid ourselves of the fear of the homosexual (our xenophobia), as we empathize with him.

## Homosexuality and the Law

Federal, state, and local government officials are being pressured to make decisions on the issue of homosexuality—the North American Conference of Homophile Organizations passed a "bill of rights" in 1968 in which they insist that candidates for elective office all take a position on homosexuality (*New York Times*, August 19, 1968). The homosexual societies hope to have a "homosexual bill of rights" enacted through pressuring these legislators, threatening that otherwise they will not vote for them and, moreover, will "trash" their campaigns. Their grandiose estimate is that over 50,000,000 homosexuals in the United States will unite to vote against any given candidate. In 1972, homosexual delegates to the Democratic National Convention in Miami promoted a plank which rightfully insisted on the lifting of persecutory laws against the homosexual but inaccurately and unfortunately tried to legitimize it as a normal form of sexuality.

It is self-evident that all human beings should have equal rights under the law. Private sexual acts by individual consenting adults usually concern only the partners themselves. If homosexuality, however, were to be practiced by 20, 30, 40, or 50 percent of the population, there would be a justified public reaction, for it would radically alter every aspect of the society in which we live.

Regulations governing the eligibility of homosexuals to serve in the armed forces should be reviewed. No one should be disqualified or discharged solely because he states that he has homosexual propensities or is a homosexual. Many homosexuals, although under considerable tension because of homosexual feelings, can serve completely satisfactorily, as I have seen from the detailed psychoanalytic reconstruction of this period in the patients' lives.

It is noteworthy to mention that even after 1967 legislation in England made it legal for consenting adults to perform homosexual acts in private,[183] the *London Times* of August 29, 1971, described the homosexual situation as follows: "Homosexuals who are *afraid* of society's penalties still live furtive sex lives in such unsuitable places as the notorious cinema and Victoria Station, public lavatories and public parks, just as they did before the 1967 Act." [Italics added] To the psychoanalyst, this is added proof that homosexuals *must* "cruise," *must* carry out a masochistic, furtive, and transient homosexual conquest, even though legal sanction has been granted to the homosexual's private life. This sanction is no more, no less, than that enjoyed by heterosexuals who also could be arrested for "lewd and lascivious behavior" were heterosexual solicitation and heterosexual sex acts carried out in public areas.

To attribute the high incidence of homosexual acts in public areas to fear of society's penalties is obviously fallacious. Sexual practices are carried out in such places precisely because it is a part of the homosexual pattern. The motivation is not fear of social reprisal; homosexuals have no other choice as they are often impelled by unconscious forces to seek out partners under particularly masochistic, exhibitionistic, and hazardous circumstances. Their compulsion requires secrecy.

## The "Gay" Groups

As I see it, many sociologists have been in favor of "normalizing" homosexuality or have remained silent on the issue in the face of vehement public pronouncements by Kinsey-oriented colleagues. A notable exception is Edward Sagarin, Professor of Sociology at the City College of New York. He has been especially concerned with the effects of group structure on the deviants' personal lives. He poses the question of whether any homosexual organization is really effective in helping its adherents or whether it serves only as a clever defense mechanism. Is the new self-image derived from joining these organizations based on a real desire to pursue legitimate goals or does their rhetoric allow them to silence public censure while pursuing "personal fetishes unhampered"?[137]

The "joiners" believe that their goal will be achieved only to the extent that people think of them as normal although nonconformist. Thus, the word "homophile" is used as a euphemism for the harsher (or, rather, more accurate) "homosexual," for homosexuals often do not "love" other men at all. According to Sagarin, it is almost impossible for an observer to fail to note the divergence between the homosexual's romantic fantasies and his life experience. On the one hand, he projects (particularly through the homophile movement) an image of romantic love; on the other, he shares knowledge of an extraordinary amount of male prostitution and compulsive searching for partners (or *cruising*, as this activity is called). Homosexual pornography has a wide market; sexual interest in strangers, particularly in adolescent strangers, knows hardly any bounds. "Homophile" organizations are constantly involved with aiding people apprehended for sexual solicitation (or even sexual performances) in men's rooms. Every homosexual is aware of the ubiquity of casual relationships, ones that last a few minutes or at most one night, or the real hunger for love that meets constant frustrations, and of the fleeting nature of relationships that start with great promise and vows of fidelity.

. . . the Mattachine Society of New York is engaged in an effort to project a view of men whose bonds of affection and loyalty are similar to those that tied Damon to Pythias or that inspired Plato to write of Greek lovers dying for each other as heroes on a battlefield. Yet, this view is in sharp contradiction to the experience and knowledge of members. While the group calls for change in legal sanctions against homosexuals, it also admits that "fully half of the solicitation cases (in New York courts) occur in subway toilets." There is however, no effort to reconcile this information with the themes of romance and love.[137]

The Mattachine Society and other gay liberation groups do a vast disservice to the homosexual, the general public, and our sexual future. As Sagarin comments: "If the public considers homosexuals unchangeable, as homophile leaders believe, then it is more likely that social hostility will be alleviated. If, on the other hand, the public accepts the possibility of change, then it will continue to hold homosexuals personally responsible for continuing on their deviant path." It seems as if the individual homosexual does not matter to the group in terms of his personal pain, anguish, sorrow, bereavement, and helplessness—all of which are elements of his condition, not society's condemnation. Those homosexuals who count on the possibility of eventual reversal are deprived of all hope by these groups and may be driven to suicide.

If one denies that homosexuality is a condition amenable to change, one is then asked to believe that as a way of life it is just as desirable as heterosexuality. This may be acceptable to a member of these groups, at least for a short while, but it is still not acceptable to the many nonjoiners—by far the great majority.

The hypocrisy grows with widespread consequences. For example, some homosexual organizations deny that they are out to proselytize for homosexuality. At the same time, they assure the public that in the area of sexual behavior the "deviant way is equivalent to the accepted one." The public is urged not to educate its youth in a one-sided "prejudiced manner" in favor of heterosexuality. The Gay Liberation Front in London demands "the right to the public expression of affection allowed to heterosexuals (such as holding hands or kissing in public)" and that sex education in schools should no longer be only heterosexual (*London Times* August 29, 1971). Such demands by the gay liberation groups have profound effects on society as a whole, effects which have only just begun to surface.

It must be emphasized here that many homosexual organizations have worked long and hard in their struggle for an end to prejudice and discrimination. They have made the general public aware of their justified claims for civil rights and have begun to be instrumental in effecting long-overdue and legitimate claims. It is however when the movement is subverted by the more divisive and disruptive elements of false propagandizing that we must beware.

One unfortunate part of the misinformation being promulgated by the militant homosexual groups is that psychiatrists feel every homosexual should seek out therapy and ultimately a "conversion" to heterosexuality. This is far from the case. As psychoanalysts our aim is to help those who come to us voluntarily for help in overcoming pain and fear and opening new roads for happiness and fulfillment. Just as each individual is unique, so is the road which makes for his or her particular enrichment. Many homosexuals seek our help in dealing with a particular phobia, anxiety, or depression without any apparent desire to change their homosexuality. It must always be remembered that any use of force or coercion is completely antithetical to the psychoanalytic method.

A few examples may prove instructive. A man in his forties who has been married for twenty years, has three children and a rewarding business and social life may come into the office and reveal that he has had frequent and numerous transitory homosexual affairs throughout the years and his real sexual interest is overwhelmingly for men. If it becomes apparent that he neither wants to give up his wife and family nor does he want to give up men, then the most therapeutic course would be to alleviate his anxiety and teach him to live reconciled to both.

Many of us have encountered two middle-aged or elderly people of the same sex who have lived together for many years. They may have tried to conceal their homosexuality or may have declared it openly. If one of the partners were to seek psychiatric help for a depression, for example, I know of no psychoanalyst who would try to dissuade the patient from the bond of that particular homosexual union. Instead the complaint for which the patient sought help would be treated, and the patient hopefully would be restored to healthy functioning within the context of his or her own life.

Due to life's struggles, everyone wishes to present himself to the best advantage; when we study another person, we study someone at war, someone with interests to protect, actions to conceal, weaknesses to shield, thoughts, feelings, and motives to hide. The therapeutic situation cannot be had without a society of physicians bound by a traditional ethics which the patient understands and accepts; without belief by the patient that the doctor wants to help him and is not in any way competitive with him; and without the patient's need for help so that under pressure of his illness and in the belief that his physician will use his confidential communications only for the patient's own benefit, he will be willing to expose his fear, shame, and weakness. Since the patient deceives himself as well as others, and since he automatically hides from his own awareness the undesirable things by repressing them, a function of psychoanalysis is to bring him to express, in this confidential physician-patient relationship, not only the private thoughts, feelings, and interrelationships of which he is aware, but even (and more especially) those of which he is unaware.

# Chapter 8

# THE SEXUAL UNREASON

## The Kinsey Fallout

The Kinsey Report of 1948 has been likened in importance by some to man's radically altered view of himself initiated by Darwin's discoveries. But Kinsey's report has had, in several ways, an unfortunate and damaging delayed impact on our sexual mores.

Alfred Kinsey, a Ph.D. in zoology, made a valuable statistical survey between 1939 and 1948 of the sexual behavior of 12,000 American males. His figures are still widely cited, as there are no others of comparable scope to contradict them. In general, there is no reason to dispute his data as to *incidence*. The value of the exhaustive and informative survey was that it enumerated the manifold forms taken by a force so powerful it cannot be denied expression. The enormous public curiosity in Kinsey's figures blinded most people to some of the erroneous interpretations to which some of the figures gave rise, especially in the area of homosexuality.

Except for Lionel Trilling (in the literary arts) and some eminent psychoanalysts—especially Bergler, Kubie and Kardiner—few cared to criticize Kinsey's findings. Still fewer treated them lightly, although H. L. Mencken in his volume *Christomathy* quipped: "All this humorless document really proves is: (a) that all men lie when they are asked about their adventures in amour and (b) that pedagogues are singularly naïve and credulous creatures." There were others who condemned the material on moral rather than scientific grounds. The Kinsey conclusions and interpretations have become a banner under which the Gay Liberationists, the transsexual axis (see next chapter), and similar special pleaders have rallied, citing them as sexual gospel.

Kardiner objected to Kinsey's techniques: "Dr. Kinsey's procedure would be quite valid if he were studying variations in the anatomical structure of ants. Statistics here would show variations in biological make-up. In the study of sexual behavior, however, statistical variations are only one small part of the total study on the basis of which one could venture an interpretation. The chief reason for this is that sexual behavior is predominantly a *motivated* field. . . . The conspicuous feature of human sexuality is that it is *not governed by hormonal influences* . . . and since Kinsey does not and cannot enter upon motivation in his statistical studies . . . [they] leave us quite stranded when we try to understand what they mean."[83] [Italics added]

In 1947, the total population of the United States was 145.3 million and Kinsey stated that 37% of the male population used what he designated as the "homosexual outlet," i.e., had at least one overt homosexual experience to the point of orgasm between adolescence and old age.[87] Therefore, according to his figures, 2 out of 5 males would be considered homosexual by these "computing machine behaviorists,"[83] according to Kardiner. Kinsey announced that together with the millions of lesbians, one could arrive at a figure of approximately 50 million adults "seated in the homosexual scale of the 'heterosexual-homosexual balance.' "[87]

Although these figures were presumably compiled and presented in good faith, Kinsey himself showed a disregard for psychological factors. Bergler was sharply critical: Kinsey "takes his human guinea pigs for idealists who volunteered only for the purpose of furthering scientific research, [assuming] . . . that the chief appeal had been altruistic." But Kinsey himself in unguarded moments expressed some doubts about his volunteers. Among these, Bergler continues, "one could suspect were many homosexuals who gladly used the opportunity of proving, by volunteering, that 'everybody' has homosexual tendencies—thus seeking to diminish their own inner guilt" or sense of inferiority.[10]

Kinsey's data were valuable in that they gave us an idea of the extent and type of sexual activity engaged in by the American male and, in a subsequent study, by the American female. That is, he told us what was being done sexually and the frequency of its occurrence. He erred in attempting to interpret these statistics, a fault which is perpetuated by his followers.

Kinsey concluded that homosexuality is present in 10 per cent of all males in a persistent (obligatory) form and in 35 per cent of all males in the transitory form. He believed this was due to the fact that homosexuality is a biological variant. Kinsey invented a scale based on the incidence revealed in his own studies of homosexuality-heterosexuality, representing a continuum between homosexual and heterosexual behavior. To him this connoted that exclusive homosexuality was a normal part of the human condition, of normal sexuality, and simply existed at one end of the "homosexual-heterosexual scale." Exclusive heterosexuality was purportedly at the other end for apparently the same reason, because it was a "biological given." Conscious and unconscious motivations for the production of homosexual behavior, whether of the exclusive (obligatory) type or not, were completely disregarded. When psychodynamically trained psychiatrists refer to unconscious motives for homosexuality, the Kinsey advocates archly ask for the unconscious motives of heterosexuality. This dismissive attitude towards criticism is itself an indictment of the Kinsey method.

It is highly unlikely that biological variants reach an incidence of 10 per cent of the population or the highly inflated figure of 20 to 25 percent quoted by homosexual societies in an attempt to normalize homosexuality. But in any case, statistical studies of the type that Kinsey authored ignore the concepts of repression, unconscious mind, and of motivation. While they supply incidence rates of certain phenomena, they do so as if behavior has no connection with motivation. Since neither conscious nor unconscious motivation is even acknowledged, these studies arrive at a disastrous conclusion: that the resultant composite of sexual behavior is the *norm* of sexual behavior. The next step is to demand that the public, the law, medicine, religion, and other social institutions unquestionably accept this proposition.

Psychoanalysts comprehend the meaning of a particular act of human behavior by delving into the motivational state from which it issues. When individuals with similar behavior are analytically investigated, we then arrive at objective conclusions as to the meaning and significance of the particular phenomenon under examination. Thus is insight achieved. To form conclusions as to the specific individual meaning of an event simply because of its frequency of occurrence is to the psychoanalyst scientific folly. Only in the consultation room, using the techniques of introspective reporting and free association, protected by all the laws of medicine, will an individual, pressed by his suffering and pain, reveal the hidden (even from himself) meaning and reasons behind his acts.

Psychoanalytic treatment of homosexuals has shown that their psychosexual condition can be reversed. This condition is a developmental failure brought about by the inhibitory action of intrapsychic processes: fear, guilt, and rage, and the inhibitions secondary to them. In almost all cases of obligatory male homosexuality studied analytically, one finds that the subject in his earliest years of life was subjected to a psychologically "crushing" mother and a cold, distant, or hostile father who were instrumental in damaging the child's ability to separate from the mother at a crucial age in the individuation process (around three). As a result, an incorrect sexual identity is produced in the boy; a comparable disruption in the young girl's early development results in a faulty, distorted, and unacceptable identity as a female.

Freudian psychoanalysis is a motivational psychology. It

poses two crucial questions in all its investigations: What purpose does this piece of behavior serve? Where does it originate?

The first question is cause-searching and is our reconnaissance arm; the second is end-relating. We ask ourselves: Why does one individual insistently seek out a same-sex partner for sexual relations? Why must another practice transvestitism? Why is another able to have sexual relations only with pre-puberty children? Why does yet another require a particular article of clothing for sexual arousal? Why are particular men excited only by pornography and obscenity? Why is it that some men and women cannot function sexually unless they engage in group sex or in other forms of promiscuity? We are thus in a position, once we know the "why," to begin to search the past to discover "how" it came about and thence to treat it.

In contrast to the psychoanalytic method of investigating behavior, the only differentiation Kinsey and his followers admit to is a quantitative one. For example, among the various forms of homosexuality, Kinsey is opposed to considering a man as homosexual in whom the "heterosexual-homosexual balance" is only slightly or temporarily shifted to the homosexual side. Psychiatrically, this is incorrect, for the quantitative approach cannot replace the psychogenetic one. Bergler was fond of comparing this quantitative approach to the situation that would exist if someone invented the idea of subdividing headaches entirely according to quantitative principles, rating them from one to six according to severity. "Medically speaking, a headache is only a symptom indicating a variety of possibilities: from brain tumor to sinus infection, from migraine attack to uremia, from neurosis to high blood pressure, from epilepsy to suppressed fury. Instead of the genetic (what causes the headache) viewpoint, we would have in this new order only quantitatively varying degrees of big, middle-sized, and small headaches."[10]

The Kinsey yardstick omits differentiation of the underlying conditions. Moreover, as Bergler notes, "in the previously mentioned rating of headaches, at a specific moment a headache produced by a sinus attack could be more severe than one produced in certain stages of a brain tumor." The homosexual "outlet" covers a multitude of completely different genetic problems. Hence a genetic yardstick is *necessary* for the differentiation and therapy of the confusing and many-faceted types of human relationships.

A case in point is the homosexual who never resorts to homosexual acts but whose sexual life is concentrated exclusively on masturbation with homosexual fantasies. Using the Kinsey yardstick of number of homosexual contacts, we would say this man was not a homosexual, but medically, we would be completely in error. Careful clinical examination would, in all likelihood, reveal that he is an obligatory homosexual of the latent type.

It must be remembered that Kinsey's study included men who were really *not* homosexual but believed that they were. They may have engaged in homosexual relations for reasons which had nothing to do with an unconscious homosexual conflict. For example, some individuals may undergo a temporary oral regression in specific situations of stress and respond to what they imagine is the "lure of the forbidden." Some individuals, under conditions of extreme dependency or in a spirit of defiance against established moral codes, may utilize homosexuality for exploitative gains and yet not be homosexual at all.

His disciples have promulgated Kinsey's thoughts and themselves proliferated as author-experts on sexual behavior and therapy without much attention from or scrutiny by the medical sciences. They have surfaced during the last fifteen years in the ferment of the widespread sexual explosion in which all value systems and sexual standards have been questioned.

Kinsey demanded the acceptance of homosexuality as a biological given to which law and prejudice should adapt itself. He spoke disparagingly of any treatment of homosexuality, even putting the word "treatment" ironically into quotation marks. He tried to capitalize upon the early pes-

simism toward psychoanalytic treatment of homosexuality—
a pessimism which has now been proven entirely unwarranted.

Kinsey buttressed his theory of a heterosexual-homosexual
scale by faulty argument: "The homosexual has been a
significant part of human sexual activity since the dawn of
history, primarily because it is an expression of capacities
that are basic in the human animal."[87] In truth, the capacity
for all organisms to become ill is basic to all human beings.
Maladaptive techniques are always pressed into service
when normal ones fail; such techniques are not justified,
only rationalized, by their own existence.

Bergler astutely sensed the danger of Kinsey's pronouncements and their insidious significance, to which he coura-
geously objected despite the unpopularity of his stand at the
time. But could Kinsey possibly "sell" America on the idea
that homosexuality was natural and normal? No one, not
even Bergler, foresaw the dimensions of the situation today.

Kinsey avoided, almost entirely, even the smallest concession to the existence of a dynamic unconscious. He called
man "the human animal," not "homo sapiens," for very definite purposes of his own. He acted as if man did not have
even an "unconscious part of his personality." By designat-
ing man the "human animal," Kinsey gives himself away,
for he is not simply stressing man's phylogenetic past but
also denying man's unique property, the cerebral cortex.
Thus he depicts man primarily as a creature without the
subtleties of conscious and unconscious motivation in the
selection of sexual objects for gratification. In Chapter 1,
I introduced the concept of man as the *beast of pride* when
he is in defeat and pain and is unable to perform at his
highest level of intellectual and emotional functioning. However, Kinsey is clearly treating our connection with our animal forebears as if man were simply an instinctual machine.
The "human animal's" sex life was determined by where one
stood on a mythical heterosexual-homosexual scale, and the
yardstick itself was exclusively "biologically conditioned."

Kinsey was very scornful of Freud. Derogatory remarks

about Freud and psychoanalysis are based mainly on ignorance, fear, and resistance, especially when they come from
laymen; they are completely indefensible when they occur
among scientists, particularly behavioral scientists. Kinsey
did not care to make it explicit that psychoanalysis had
never denied the biological substructure in human drives—
on the contrary, it had stressed them.

Furthermore, Kinsey must have known that earlier papers
on homosexuality were out of date and that the state of our
knowledge had gradually and importantly expanded. He
completely disregarded authors who wrote about these phenomena—Ernest Jones, Helene Deutsch, Sandor Lorand,
Gustav Bychowski, among others. The definitive preoedipal
theory of causation was first published by me in 1968,[152] long
after Kinsey's death, but this has never been acknowledged
by the Kinsey cult of today. My systematized preoedipal
theory of homosexuality evolved in part from the synthesis
of clinical and theoretical data and observations of many
other analysts who preceded me, analysts such as Jones,
Bychowski, Lorand, Gillespie, Nunberg, Bak and others.

Kinsey's figures and conclusions are heavily relied upon
by those who would have us accept homosexuality as simply an alternate life style. Such pronouncements of Kinsey's
as the following serve only to further complicate the public's
confusion: "Long-time relationships between two [homo-
sexual] males are notably few. Long-time relationships in
the heterosexual world would probably be less frequent than
they are if there were no social custom or legal restraints to
enforce continued relationship in marriage. But without
such outside pressure to preserve homosexual relations, and
with personal and social conflicts continually disturbing
them, relationships between males rarely survive the first
disagreement. The stability of heterosexual love relationships is only a concession to social customs."[87]

These statements show a grandiose disregard of the psychological facts of life. In reality, the unconscious motivations in heterosexual and homosexual relationships are totally

different. For example, Bergler, with whose conclusions I am in complete agreement, states that the homosexual's

> compensatory aggression towards the mother (projected on the homosexual partner) results in the repetitive tendency to discard the partner after using him. . . . Nowhere is the impersonal part of the human relationship so predominant as in homosexuals, as visible in the fact that some of them have masturbatory activities in comfort stations without even knowing or looking at their partners. . . . As far as homosexuals remaining together for any length of time, their quarrels, especially in jealousy, surpass everything that occurs, even in the worst heterosexual relationships. They simply act out of the mechanism of injustice collecting. . . . [In heterosexual relationships] the tender element (completely disregarded by Kinsey) plays an important part, especially in its unconscious connotations. How one can describe the phenomenon of human sexual relations and at the same time omit tender love is not quite comprehensible. It is as if somebody described a sunset without mentioning the colors. The omission is not a small one; the whole description becomes worthless.[11]

## Masters's Folly

Early in 1972, when Dr. William H. Masters of St. Louis announced to the nation's press that homosexuality is a "natural" and by direct implication normal sexual act or sexual condition, he raised the status of the anus to the level of the vagina (*New York Times,* November 18, 1971). What was, until then, a purely excretory organ had become a genital one—by decree. It seems that Masters, a competent but psychoanalytically uninformed physician, had become an easy convert to the ideology of the Indiana-based social psychologists belonging to the Kinsey cult.

There are serious implications in Masters's pronouncement. For one, implicit in it is the negation of entire spheres of human knowledge—the findings of psychoanalysis regarding sexual development and the origin of sexual deviations. Second, his pronouncement provides homosexuals with the false comfort of a rationalization for the tragic loss of the opportunity to engage in every way in the male-female pattern of life. Despite this rationalization, which is supposed to soothe the pain and anguish of homosexuals, they remain no less vulnerable to the warring intrapsychic forces which propel them into homsexual practices and produce the anxieties that so adversely dominate their lives.

This inner conflict is taking place every moment in the troubled life of the homosexual whether his homosexuality is designated "normal" or "abnormal." Since Masters has no experiences in treating homosexuals psychiatrically, he does not realize that the vast majority of them (despite what militant homosexual groups would have us believe) do not wish to be homosexual—regardless of whether the wish is conscious or unconscious. Their lives are characterized by intermittent desperation and the hope that psychiatry, luck, someone, or something will rescue them and relieve their exclusion from rewarding and meaningful relationships.

Now Masters promises to "help" homosexuals by implementing their proficiency in homosexual techniques in order to have better orgasms with their same-sex partners. Through instructing them in this way, he is, in effect, "burying" them. By citing such chemical discoveries as the "differences" of circulating hormones in the blood between homosexuals and nonhomosexuals, Masters demonstrates his lack of psychiatric knowledge of the dynamics of homosexual behavior. We have long known that conclusions based on chemical assays of androgen levels of small groups of homosexuals and heterosexuals are useless. (Masters utilized the erroneous Kinsey scale, perpetuating earlier mistakes by dividing the population into exclusive homosexuals at one end, exclusive heterosexuals at the other and the remainder in between the two.) The presence or absence of a chemical is often a *consequence* of whatever activity one is engaged in, not its cause, Furthermore, its replacement cannot alter sexual-object choice. The latter is a complex matter involving the cerebral cortex at the motivational level of behavior. Hormone levels can differ with the strength of constitutional sex drive in all individuals, but they do not influence the choice of a same-sex or opposite-sex partner, which is learned behavior.

The dismal proposition set before the homosexuals, if Masters's view is to be accepted, is for the homosexual to vaginalize his anus and prepare himself to fulfill the female "pull" function in the push-pull principle of sexual intercourse. (See Chapter 2.) To the majority of the nation's homosexuals, this is a horrifying specter and a staggering and tragic blunder on Dr. Masters's part, especially in view of the remarkable research he has achieved on the *physiology* of the human sexual response.[74]

Moreover, I believe his announcement could not have come at a worse time. The public was beginning to inquire and learn about sexual deviations and as a result was displaying more compassion toward and understanding of them. Any totalitarian regime of the future could readily seize upon this misinformation in order to pronounce homosexuals "different" on an organic basis and permanently seal their fate.

Proclaiming sexual deviations to be "normal" automatically means nothing can or need be done to help or change them. There is already untold confusion and despair at this harsh and mistaken view. We will be turned back to an era when the homosexual and any other sexual deviant was beyond the ministrations of the medical profession. In time the sexually different will be thrown to the unpredictable and unscientific reactions of an untrained and unenlightened public. For Masters and his associates are, in fact, consigning homosexuals to the limbo from which psychoanalysis nearly succeeded in rescuing them.

Masters and Johnson are not the only ones to fall victim to the delayed effects of the Kinsey fallout. Psychologist John Money and his staff at Johns Hopkins, the prime movers for transsexual operations in this country, have espoused the belief that Kinsey was right and that homosexuality and transvestitism are not psychological but are biological variants, therefore normal psychologically. This misinformed attitude has spread over the nation and dominates the thinking of numerous gender-identity clinics at medical institutions.

## The Erotic Forecasts of Alexander Comfort

Paradise will soon be here on the planet Earth, according to Alexander Comfort. Dr. Comfort, a biologist, is Associate Fellow at the Center for the Study of Democratic Institutions in Santa Barbara, California; head of the Aging Research Institute of the University College, London; and author of the popular best seller *The Joy of Sex.*[27]

While Comfort's remarkable book on sexual technique and the enjoyment of sex is a valid piece of work, his most recent assessment of our erotic future, described in an article, "Sexuality in a Zero Growth Society,"[26] is most disturbing. His position is based on a mistaken and ignorant foundation: "since zero population growth will be an overriding social objective," the entire meaning of sex and sexual behavior will and must undergo drastic revisions and a "new game with different rules will appear." He writes as though he had just discovered the pleasure-potential of sex. He announces that "contraception has for the first time wholly separated the three human uses of sex—sex as parenthood, sex as total intimacy between two people ('relational' sex), sex as physical play ('recreational' sex)." Sexual relations have always been practiced for their "recreational/relational" motivation; the reproductive function was always a co-motivation.

It is fallacious to assert that because we now have effective contraceptive techniques, nonreproductive motivations for sexual intercourse are any more powerful in the minds of men and women than heretofore. The nonreproductive pleasure aims of sex have been paramount since time immemorial. It is probably more accurate to say that nature, somehow, saw fit to remove reproduction from the caprice of man's ignorant will; to assure the survival of the species and the future evolution of life, the act of reproduction was generously coated with pleasure.

Comfort predicts in his "new game with different rules" that the concept of the family will be radically altered. He characterizes this vital foundation unit of life as neurotic, a "totally self-sufficient couple-relationship, involving the ideal surrender of identity and of personal selfhood. . . ." Adamantly he asserts that young people today "see this" and will deal with life in "more realistic" terms. He feels that the pill has changed things so that not only men but women can now "enjoy sex" at all three levels (as if they hadn't for thousands of years). He exclaims that the "fantasy-concept of total one-to-one sufficiency has let us down."

Predicting a utopia in which "if we pass the test, we may evolve into a universal human family in which all three types of sex have their place, . . . in which we are all genuinely kin, and in which all but the most unrealistic inner needs can be met in one family or another," Comfort forgets that most needs of most people are unrealistic most if not all of the time, except in those who have reached and maintain an unusual level of maturity.

Comfort feels the beginning of institutionalizing ritual spouse exchange is a "more honest, and a better bet anthropologically" than marriage. Proprietary sexual attitudes will have to cease. With dash and daring he predicts but still retracts: "Unless the result disturbs children and leads to a backlash generation, the genuine insight present in 'swinging' by the bored and the unrealized could expand into something far more like institutionalized socio-sexual openness."

To the psychoanalyst who deals daily with the problems which Comfort takes so lightly, his theoretical propositions would seem farcical were they not already in vogue and being practiced by some segments of our population, aided and augmented by the pseudoscience of those with Comfort's views. For he states:

> This process, so far as it has gone, would have been impossible without a gradual change in attitude toward, and anxiety about, bisexuality. Mate-sharing, both psychoanalytically, and in primate ethology, reveals a surrogate sexual relation between males—expressed covertly so far in the gang's night out and the attraction of the prostitute or "shared" woman, acceptable substitutes for overt male-male contacts because they are covert. The potential for more open bisexual contacts is greatly increased by two-couple activity. Men tend still to be disturbed by this, but women, who are in general less anxious about their bisexual potential, often embrace the opportunity with male encouragement. In fact, judging from primates, the state of sharing with another male, which reinforces individual dominance, could well help rather than hinder the heterosexuality of anxious people—dominance anxiety plays a large part in the suppression of heterosexual drives in most persons who regard themselves as constitutionally homosexual.[26]

This quote seems to contain by far, the largest number of errors in all of Comfort's debatable assertions. The contention that men who engage in intercourse with the same prostitute are, in fact, having hidden homosexual relations with each other (not consistently the case by any means) and the contention that women wish to have sexual relations with each other and welcome this opportunity in two-couple or multi-couple group sex are both utterly without foundation. Most women who engage in homosexual contact under such circumstances and are not otherwise homosexuals view the activity with deep disdain and participate only at the insistence of their men (see Chapter 4). Furthermore, to conclude about them, as does Comfort, that there is such a condition as "constitutional" homosexuality is to display ignorance of current psychiatric literature.

Comfort goes so far as to believe that homosexuality and

group sex will reinstate the kinship of men and women. In essence, he is leaving out the entire psychodynamics of overt obligatory homosexuality and its origins in the earliest years of life.

His view of the future of sex includes a time when romantic sex will be considered only a product of fear of rejection. He regards attempts to transcend jealousy through wife-swapping or of greater tolerance of extramarital affairs as realistically meeting the needs of couples and individuals. All this supermarital sex would mark the end of the mutual proprietorship, physical or emotional, which he feels has so often characterized human sexual relationships in the past—neurotic and immature relationships, in his opinion.

To him human love has always been found unsatisfactory in every society. "Certainly none of the past fictions embodied in our stereotypes of male and female sex roles, of totally exclusive love or even of central parenthood can readily persist unaltered." Rejection of the "fictions" of love is fine for Comfort and perhaps for a race of robots, but not for human beings governed by certain basic unconscious psychodynamic laws. No matter the degree of self-control and their achievement of functioning at the group membership level, people are vulnerable to reversion to the beast of prey, the forces of false pride and brute emotion which lie beneath the topmost layers of mind and spirit.

Comfort's version of Paradise will be a place where "pair relationships are . . . less permanent, . . . and in which settled couples engage openly in a wide range of sexual relations with friends, with other couples, and with third parties . . . , without prejudice to the primacy of their own relationship." Such a pattern is emerging in the United States and is beginning to become explicit. He feels it will not devalue relationships; it will only deprive them of "neurotic compulsion."

The fly in the ointment, however, becomes apparent when one considers the political implications of such behavior. Comfort feels men and women will really "behave themselves" if they are given unbridled sexual license. In my opinion the inevitable consequences of such license eradicating the bonds of the romantic pair, marriage, family, and the community would be a vacuum in which a government, a superstate, would then seize the opportunity to govern the behavior of its individuals sexually, allowing them Comfort's "freedom." It would be of course in the interest of any future dictatorial power to foster the sexual egalitarianism which Comfort envisages.

The kingdom of the orgasm has arrived since the pill has been the key to unlock it. Psychological help is equated with unfettered gratification of the instincts. The ego (the self) is involved only to the extent that its hold over instinctual expression must be broken. This is the sexual future which Comfort and others predict—all too eager to bring back the primacy of instinct. But this is no mere fantasy. It is happening everywhere, from small towns in Kansas to New York City and throughout the world.

But will the kingdom of the orgasm demolish the house of the ego? Psychiatrists have learned to deal with the ego— helping it in its defense and expression, in its struggle against conflicting desires, tyrannical conscience, and the forces of repression and inhibition. It is tempting, of course, to play with the Promethean forces of the unconscious for many and variegated motivations. These may be political, instinctual; they may arise from poor psychology, for the mechanization of all things including the sexual instinct, and for the ever-present wish of orgastic pleasure. The fate of the orgasm, like the fate of the atom, is in man's hands. It would be folly to assume, because the one (like the other) is a "natural" phenomenon, that it will necessarily take its "natural" course. Man can manipulate and mismanage and even denature almost anything he puts his mind to.

# Chapter 9

# SEX-TRANSFORMATION SURGERY

## *The Genital "Crucifiers"*

Dr. Socarides:

I saw your name in the *San Francisco Chronicle*. You claim to have analyzed a "so-called transsexual" and warn about the big mistake of trying to make women out of male nature. I consider it my duty to support you and help you the best I can to save other human beings the agony I am living through.

I am going to repeat more or less—the words I wrote to Dr. X. I told him how long and grey were my days after the trip to Casablanca.

. . . Not many human beings were as happy as I felt. Probably that's why I trusted—or pressed—my luck and thought everything, once more, would be for the better.

My male sexual organs are gone! Dr. Y performed "in cold blood" on me one of those horrible mutilations. My so-called artificial vagina entrance looks like a ring of empty scrotum. I will have to live, if I have the courage, with this monstrosity. My male sexual organs can't be priced at this moment. If all the gold in the world had been offered to me—with full knowledge of what the operation was—for them I would have never accepted such a bargain. I don't see the moment when that open wound that has to be treated—dilation—to remain open, will close. It's incredible to me that these operations are being done officially in the U.S.A.

If I had seen one of those operations—Frankensteins!— I wouldn't have ever consented to it! Dr. X is very smart. In his book he publishes some pictures but not the essential one! A photo of the "so-called artificial entrance." I have many letters from him encouraging me even though he never saw me. When I asked him if he considered the operation worthy he "played foxes." If I had seen or known this! How can a human being do this to another? I never expected anything as perfect as a woman's vagina but this "revolting thing" I don't dare to look upon myself. It was beyond my expectations.

Dr. Socarides, can you imagine my situation? I will have to live with something that just gives me nausea as part of my nature where before there was something so healthy and beautiful—my God! *I paid to be crucified.*

Ignorance and credulity are going to hurt, and already have, many honest and worthy people. Not long ago I saw in the *San Francisco Chronicle* a poor man crying after what they did to him in Denmark. Why did nobody warn me?

I am ready to tolerate pictures taken—without publicity of my name—to be shown to future victims. My body looks in every sense as a man's body. I was not treated with hormones or through electrolysis. That made very little difference to Dr. X. You, and the psychiatrists who want to help and stop this infamy, should put all the emphasis on opening the eyes of the victim.

What am I going to do now? How much is left of my life? Today I am nothing but the victim of a society that refused me help and respect. I never did anything against society or the law. I was so quiet! That is the kind of person that usually gets hurt!

No surgery can possibly produce anything that resembles a female vagina. The operation is a theft. It is nothing but an open wound. It needs dilation to keep it open and if dilated too much becomes useless for intercourse. Such an open wound lacks protective membranes and bleeds under pressure. What transsexual would dare to lay in bed—with full light—with his legs wide open? What man would tol-

erate such a spectacle? A piece of phallus with an open
wound below and a ring of scrotum hanging is all it is.
Who calls that an artificial vagina is nothing but a bandit
looking for ignorant and credulous people to exploit them.

This letter, complete with the writer's name and address,
postmarked March 22, 1969, reached me after press reports
of my study on change-of-sex surgery, "The Plaster-of-Paris
Man," was presented before the American Psychoanalytic
Association in December 1968.[156] I have reproduced it here
so that the reader may sense directly the anguish involved
in this situation.

Before proceeding further in the exploration of this
phenomenon, a definition of "transsexualism" is in order.
It is a psychiatric syndrome characterized by an intense,
insistent, and overriding wish or desire for sexual transformation into a person of the opposite sex.

Transformation is to be effected through direct surgical
alteration of the external and internal sexual apparatus and
secondary sex characteristics of the body, and indirectly
through the administration of endocrinological preparations.
The subject's conviction that he is "basically" a person of
the opposite sex may be semidelusional or delusional in
quality. It may be part of an underlying schizophrenic psychosis. If not, it is always based on a failure to attain a definitive male or female identity in accordance with anatomy.

Transsexuals display behavior concomitant with their
desire for change, behavior imitative of that of the opposite
sex. There are alterations in dress, activities, attitudes, choice
of sexual partner—all are a part of the desperate attempt to
strengthen the wished-for transformation. Most of all, these
individuals insist upon transformation, sometimes even to
the point of self-inflicted multilative acts.[154]

Efforts at gender transmutation or sexual transformation
through endocrinological or surgical techniques began in the
early 1930s. However, only in the last decade has systematic
information on these experiments become available to behavioral scientists. Still the information remains incomplete,

fragmentary, contradictory, and confusing. Many of the questions brought by these procedures raise issues about the biological roots of human behavior and call for careful assessment and reassessment of psychiatry's diagnostic tools and therapeutic endeavors. They warrant relentless and penetrating evaluations of theoretical formulations on the interrelationship between body structure and psychological process. Such questions also challenge diagnostic classifications of the sexual disorders and should lead ultimately to in-depth psychoanalytic research into the origin of these psychological disturbances. This is the job of the psychoanalytically trained physician—not of the surgeon.

Transsexualism is a psychological condition; a transsexual is a *biologically normal* person who wishes to change his sexual identity into a person of the opposite sex. Many of us would call his disease in its extremest form an iatrogenic disease (born of physicians). The *strictly morphological* changes have been possible only since modern methods of plastic surgery and improved endocrinologic techniques have made possible the construction of a simulated vagina and breast enlargement. The artificial vagina is usually very short; like all incisions it tends to close up on itself, needs frequent dilations, and often bleeds, and the area is subject to much cheloid formation (overgrowth of scar tissue). The "changes" are *strictly morphological*—a microscopic examination of the scraping of the buccal epithelium of the inner side of the cheek of such a person after surgery and hormone injection reveals the same chromosomal pattern with which he was born.

Endocrine preparations can alter the secondary sex characteristics such as distribution of fat and hair, texture of skin, etc. Until recently, surgical attempts to construct functional penises for women undergoing "transformation" have proven highly unsuccessful, but, of course, breasts and internal organs are *removed* quite easily.

According to W. St. C. Symmers of the Department of Pathology, Charing Cross Hospital, London: "Whatever the forces are that drive some individuals to procure the outward physical appearance of the sex that they were not born to, the normal man and woman tend to be shocked on discovering the extent that others will go to in the search for sex metamorphosis. A sense of shock may be a natural reaction . . . but it should surely be tempered through pity. . . . Many must feel sympathy . . . and perhaps something of anger [at] men and women prostituting medical skills,"[168] Symmers's paper presents two postsurgical cases, both of which ended in death due to cancer of the breast in men whose hormonal balance had been massively upset by castration and the administration of estrogens.

The actualization of the wish to become a person of the opposite sex is a contemporary development, but the wish itself is ancient. There are numerous examples in literature of man's compelling urge to make this transformation—for example, the Emperor Caligula and the French Ambassador to Siam under Louis XV.

It is not reasonable to take an individual who is basically suffering from a *psychic* disorder in which he believes himself to be intrinsically a person of the opposite sex and attempt to "change" him by irreversible surgery. His irrational conviction that he is, for example, a "female trapped in a male body" is a consequence of deep disturbances in body-image formation and body ego. These difficulties arise in the earliest years of life, before the age of three, during the separation-individuation phase of development. Instead of the boy's attaining identity in accordance with anatomy, as in normal child development, there is a continuation of primary feminine identification with the mother, along with feelings of being feminine and lacking in masculinity.

These phenomena arise out of severe psychic conflicts prior to the oedipal phase (age three to five). When this failure in emotional development becomes manifest, it must be treated by psychological measures, preferably by psychoanalysts medically qualified to recognize the complex relationships and distinctions mentioned above. It is best treated, as with any disorder of such early onset, in the first decade of life.

The fact is that semantics cannot substitute for psychological treatment of the transsexual. The caricature of femininity to which surgery gives rise cannot begin to offer any solution to the beset individual who has a highly distorted image of the woman's role he aspires to experience. He is most often preoccupied with ideas of glamour and what he believes to be unending sexual and social pleasures and advantages. He fails to see and wishes to ignore any mundane or demanding responsibilities, or the real nature of being a woman.

A rather horrifying account of the confusion which follows acting out of such a fantasy appeared July 22, 1971, in the *Bernardsville* (New Jersey) *News:*

> A Cedar High School music teacher who underwent surgery to change his sex from male to female this spring, and kept the knowledge secret from colleagues, is now discussing future teaching plans with the Board of Education. The teacher is 52-year-old Paula Miriam Grossman, previously known as Paul Monroe Grossman, and whether she will continue to teach here is a matter that may not be disclosed until the Board's next meeting on Thursday, August 12th. . . . [Grossman is] a music teacher on tenure with 31 years' experience, 14 of which have been in the Bernard Township School System. . . . The operation is reported to have taken place in the Wickersham Hospital, New York City, in March, and Mrs. Grossman was absent from her duties as a vocal music teacher in the fifth and sixth grade elementary school for about one month. When she returned, she continued to dress as a male and apparently aroused no suspicion. Near the end of April, she told school superintendent M. D. Headington about the change and indicated she expected to teach next year as usual. The top administrator was reportedly stunned by the revelation. . . .

Four months later, "Mrs." Grossman appeared as a guest on a syndicated television program with two other post-surgery transsexuals, all in female garb and hairstyles. He

revealed a long history of transvestitism and a lifelong desire
to "be a woman." Although married and the father of three
children, he had decided to have his genitalia removed and
a vagina constructed.

Decidedly masculine in both body proportions and tone of
voice, "Mrs." Grossman explained that he had had neither
female hormone preparations to enlarge the breasts nor
electrolysis to remove facial hair, as had the other guests. He
could not afford any payments beyond the $6,000 already paid
the doctors, which constituted his life savings. Furthermore,
he planned to go on living with his wife of twenty years and
said that their children would continue to call him "Daddy."
Unlike the other guests, he had no interest in sexual experience with men.

Grossman's remarks were not the most bizarre on the
program. One of the other guests, whose surgery had been
performed in Casablanca, said he knew a doctor, in a country
he would not name, who offered further surgery to trans-
plant internal generative organs so that he could eventually
give birth to a child.

The third guest, in great discomfort because he had just
left the hospital following genital surgery, explained that
this was the culmination of a long series of operative procedures: rhinoplasty, "elevation of the cheekbones," and removal of a protruding Adam's apple as well as silicone
breast implants.

Transsexual news becomes more and more disturbing. A
news item in the *New York Post* on October 9, 1969, reported
the birth of a daughter to "Dawn Hall Simmons," the former
Gordon Langley Hall. "When Mrs. Simmons announced
three weeks ago that she was pregnant, doctors at Johns
Hopkins Hospital in Baltimore, where the sex-change surgery
took place last year, said, 'It's definitely impossible' for Mrs.
Simmons to become pregnant. In an interview at her home,
Mrs. Simmons said, 'I believe that God is higher than medical science and that's my explanation.' " She said the baby
was still in the hospital and no photographs of the infant
were available at the time; nothing further has been re-

ported. Clearly childbirth is impossible for a transformed transsexual. Still the article demonstrates the severe distortion of reality that is often so grossly apparent in these patients.

In a midtown Manhattan proprietary hospital, there are many men in various stages of "feminization" pre- and post-surgery. For, a minimum of $5,000 one can board a private bus departing from Park Avenue and Eighty-Sixth Street in New York traveling directly to the airport, returning to the departure point a month later with a "change of sex." This is the "group rate." Preliminary to this, there are costly and frequent visits to designated physicians for daily hormone administration.

Ten to fifteen years ago there were rumors of clandestine change-of-sex operations performed in the United States for large sums of money. The rationalization was then put forth that some United States hospitals finally became involved with sex-change operations because of the botched-up jobs done in secrecy, both here and abroad. As Herbert Gant reported in *Psychiatric News:* "From repair work to complete operation is a big leap, but a few hospitals finally made the theoretical jump, reasoning [according to John Money, Ph.D., psychologist at Johns Hopkins and a leader of the transsexual movement] that the condition of faulty gender identity as much justified surgical intervention as . . . a partial castration from an improperly done operation."[53]

At the present time, the leading medical institutions in the United States involved in gender-identity clinics and sex-transformation surgery are: Johns Hopkins (the first hospital in the United States officially to provide the surgery), the University of Minnesota, and the University of Washington in Washington State. Others have gender identity clinics but do not perform surgery, such as the University of California at Los Angeles and the University of Michigan. Wayne State University in Michigan is proceeding most cautiously in the psychiatric study of gender-role confusion.

Dr. Richard Green, Director of the Gender Identity Clinic

at UCLA, stated that about 100 (university-based) sex-change operations had been done in the United States as of 1970, and 200 to 300 in foreign countries since 1953. Another source, Dr. Howard W. Jones of Johns Hopkins, reported that his hospital had performed sex-change operations on 34 persons in a six-year period (1966–72) and the Gender Identity Clinic there had a backlog of 200 to 300 applicants for the procedure (*San Juan Star*, October 14, 1972). It is amazing that Dr. Jones's waiting list isn't longer when one can turn on the television and hear the following report.

On a recent Thanksgiving day a local television station sent a reporter out on the streets of Manhattan to ask passersby what they were thankful for. One young man replied without hesitation: "I'm thankful that I live in the United States and will soon have my change-of-sex operation. This is the only country in the world where it is legal now." But the statistics are only a partial indication of the extent of the problem.

I question all these statistics because they do not include operations in private hospitals which have been sparked by the prestige given the surgery by renowned medical teaching institutions. It is difficult to ascertain how many individuals have been operated on and where; probably they number in the thousands. It is reported that there is a ratio of three or four males to every one female who wants to change sex. In February, 1969, Johns Hopkins Hospital stopped the procedure, subject to the findings of follow-up studies of former patients. This temporary cessation of the surgery at Hopkins also followed the presentation of my paper "The Plaster-of-Paris Man" and its nationwide coverage by the news media as well as adverse comments on sex-change surgery published by Dr. Lawrence    Kubie, former Professor of Psychiatry at Yale.

On October 29, 1969, I attended a meeting at the New York Academy of Medicine when the Johns Hopkins sex-reassignment team presented a report on its work. They revealed that the procedure on the female had at that point been suspended because of the difficulty in fashioning and constructing a functioning penis for the female. "The transformation of a woman to a man requires a complex, three-stage course of surgery that takes at least six months to a year. The breasts and internal sex organs are removed. A scrotum is made from labial tissue and filled with plastic 'testicles.' A penis is created in stages; a skin graft from the abdominal wall is built into a tube that hangs down to enclose an artificial urethra. Finally, the clitoris is embedded in the artificial penis, so that capacity for orgasm is retained. At best, the penis is not very large or realistic, and it cannot become erect; to penetrate a vagina, it must be given artificial support."[85] The creation of Mary Shelley's Frankenstein monster pales in comparison to this grotesque spare-parts, Tinker-Toy type of surgery practiced on living, suffering, and desperate human beings.

What are the reasons behind the toleration of such legalized castration, especially in the context of the first principle of medicine: *Primum Non Nocere* (Above all, do no harm)? The answer derives from the social, cultural, and psychological upheaval of our time. The confusion of sex roles and a profound current of anti-Freudianism pervade the country. The unconscious factors in the production of the severe psychological disturbance which leads to the desire to change sex are virtually denied by those physicians who participate in the procedures. To "change" men into women and vice versa as Circe turned men into beasts may very well feed an unresolved, unconscious infantile omnipotence in those who perform the surgical operations.

This medical chaos continues because of the misconception that the eradication of sex-role differences and their facile reassignment will bring man greater happiness. In consequence, life is treated cheaply and sex is treated as one of its cheapest commodities.

Dr. Robert Stoller, psychoanalyst and professor at UCLA, has carried out successful psychoanalytic therapy of boys who suffered from gender-identity conflicts and has contributed a great deal to the literature on the advisability of such procedures.[165] It was gratifying to receive a personal communication from him, dated May 14, 1969, in which he expressed his new views on the origin, nature, and meaning of transsexualism:

> All the information I've collected recently shows that the small number of very feminine patients we see here, whom we call transsexuals, seem to be that way because of a collection of forces, all *psychological* [italics added], which unhappily come together in one family to make the little boy so feminine. . . . We have no evidence whatsoever that any special biological force is at work in these children, and all of my publications in recent years on the subject attempted to show the data behind that belief. . . . I have felt . . . that it is the interpersonal, preoedipal, intrafamilial conditions that produce transsexualism. . . . The data you have and the data I have powerfully suggest that whatever "biological force" (a very vague term that I have specifically used in order not to pretend to be precise) might be demonstrated in the future in humans, they do not contribute specifically to such things as marked femininity in males or masculinity in females, do not produce homosexuality, and will not play a part in treatment aimed at modifying aberrations in masculinity and femininity.[166]

When psychiatrists are opposed to such surgical mutilations, they are accused of being opposed only because of their own "castration fear"—as if the very existence of this fear on a universal level did not already indict the operation. For instance, psychologist John Money of Johns Hopkins remarks, "I am constantly vexed in listening to our critics and deciding who is the rational physician and who is the man reacting to castration fears."[53] To accuse psychoanalysts who refuse to participate in penis amputations of suffering from castration anxiety is both laughable and outrageous, for the advocacy of transsexual surgery reflects both the dehumanization of sex and the lack of respect for the sexual dignity of the individual.

## Victor-Valerie:
## The Plaster-of-Paris Man

The following is a brief case history of a transsexual patient who underwent psychoanalysis with me for a period of six months. If the language in this section seems somewhat dryly scientific and clinical, it is because it is just that—a psychoanalytic case history.

When the general public first became acquainted with the transsexual phenomenon some twenty years ago with the highly publicized case of Christine Jorgenson, it then semed a uniquely bizarre and mysterious event. Now however, television interviews, magazine articles and recently, several books, Jan Morris's *Conundrum* in particular, have acquainted us with many more of these cases. In interviews, individuals who have undergone the surgery unanimously attest to their long struggle of having to live as one sex "trapped in the body" of the opposite sex. They appear to be genuinely fulfilled and grateful to medical science for now having brought them the transformation they long awaited. On the surface the case usually is vastly oversimplified— often presented like the relief someone would realistically feel after a piece of corrective orthopedic surgery designed to restore normal functioning and movement. But we must remember that this is strictly a surface presentation of the outward manifestations of a profound psychic disorder. It is in the hope of revealing the *underlying* conflicts and conditions which drive transsexuals to seek surgery that I present the case of Victor-Valerie.[156]

My patient, to whom I have given the name of Victor-Valerie, was a prototype of the transsexual, neither an intersex nor a hypogonadal individual. In other words, he suffered from no embryological defect nor did his endocrine glands malfunction. Victor-Valerie is the first case of transsexualism to have undergone psychoanalytic investigation.

Victor-Valerie was a gifted young research student of twenty who lived only for the day when he would have his sex-change operation. He reluctantly agreed to undergo psychoanalysis with the provision that his parents would then reconsider their opposition to surgery. He appeared at our first appointment as a rather attractive man, looking somewhat younger than his age, and speaking softly, courteously, and with no particular distinction. He was pale, slender, of average height, and his body movements were feline and graceful.

Midway in treatment, he informed me that he had regularly been receiving hormone injections during the psychoanalysis, contrary to our original agreement. At the end of six months, when he reached the age of twenty-one, he forced his parents to acknowledge defeat, and with his father's reluctant concurrence, triumphantly withdrew from treatment. However, of extreme importance is the legacy Victor left to psychoanalysis in understanding transsexual behavior: free association, fantasies, memories, dreams, and a historical reconstruction of the incidents responsible for his transsexualism.

His first attempt to directly feminize himself by wearing women's clothes and makeup in private began at nineteen, when a homosexual affair with a teacher ended because the teacher would not accept his feminine behavior. There was, however, unconscious interest in sex transformation before that time. He had begun to feel that his homosexual affairs were different from those of other homosexuals because he was "really a woman." He tentatively decided to reinforce this belief by anatomical change. A "revelation" during an LSD experience confirmed to him that he was indeed "a female caught in a male body." He thereupon started facial electrolysis to remove all signs of a beard as well as hormone therapy to induce breast enlargement, ingesting double the prescribed dosage whenever he could manage to obtain additional supplies. Five months before entering psychoanalysis with me, he attempted a self-vasectomy without anesthesia. "I tried to cut my scrotum open, I shaved the scrotal sac with a razor blade, and I started to cut the scrotum. The first cut was not painful as the blade was very sharp, but then it started to sting. I stopped. . . . I feel I have a tumor between my legs. The tumor is my scrotum and my penis. Cutting the vas deferens would stop the sperm from forming and cause the testicles to atrophy."

He had been in psychotherapy at brief intervals since the age of fourteen, due to homosexuality and severe depression, having twice attempted suicide during late adolescence. He was expelled from college at the height of an LSD experiment which had produced uncontrollable crying spells and "bottomless" depressions.

Victor was the youngest of three siblings with a brother eight years older and a sister four years older. They were a middle-class family who enjoyed considerable financial status through the father's outstanding business talents. The patient had been born and brought up in a suburban area of a large southwestern city. By the age of four, he was aware of his father's frequent and severe depressive states, and recalls that his mother would leave him with the father in an effort to alleviate the latter's depression. He would get into bed with his father, cuddle close to him, and feel "great love" for him. Beginning at two years of age, there were severe oral conflicts which were expressed in the rejection of solid foods. This lasted until the age of eight or nine, and the symptom recurred periodically when he was extremely nervous. "I used to chew meat and not swallow it. I would spit it out and put it on the plate. And I drank cans and cans of nutriment, cold drinks not hot drinks. I was never breast-fed. I feel somehow that I was deprived early. I would eat no solids whatsoever and I could not stand milk products. My mother would force me to swallow solid foods, chew them up, lumps of cold meat, sometimes in a restaurant. I couldn't swallow one. I have no comprehension of chewing and swallowing. That's weird. It is difficult for me to even do it now. I sometimes have to subsist on liquid foods for days or months. Now and then I get a craving to chew. Even now, however, there is a long period of abstinence from chewing. If I do eat meat now, I eat it raw."

In psychoanalytic language, this young man suffered from an intense oral fixation, evidenced by his inability to eat solid foods, a craving for liquids, and the "weird" feeling of "no comprehension" of the act of swallowing. He craved oral satisfaction but his fear of solid food, which symbolized to him the solid (impure, dangerous, destructive, poisonous) maternal body, caused him to avoid it.

Throughout the first three years of life, his dread of the female body was in conflict with his deep attachment to it. He could not bear to be separated from his mother, clinging to her and screaming incessantly when she was absent.

By the age of five, his mother—who already complained about his feminine traits—would call him a "sissy" and make fun of his "girlishness." Homosexual relations with his older brother began at age seven, and lasted for a period of seven years. They regularly involved hugging and kissing and anal intercourse, in which Victor played the passive role. During this period of life, everything seemed to take place in a dream: "I can't understand this hazy period. It lasted until I was about twelve. In the sixth grade, it was quite strong. In prepuberty, I kind of woke up. I was nothing up to that time. It seems to me I never matured sexually. . . . Everything moved, however, from seven to twelve, as if I were in a dream. I couldn't tell dream from reality. By the age of thirteen, I knew there was something really different with me, that I was not like everyone else."

Throughout childhood, he was "bored with everything" except books. He felt that his sister was not a "true member" of the family, perhaps she had been adopted, thereby overcoming his sibling rivalry with her; he liked her best and he wanted to be just like her. Speaking of his parents, Victor says, "When my father is in a bad mood, I simply smile at him now, although it would have upset me terribly in the past." His mother was reared in foster homes and he dwelled on this fact. "She must have been terribly deprived. She had no sex explained to her as a child, and she has always felt that men only wanted sex from women. She told me this at an early age. She married my father at sixteen. To her, sex is not a thing to be given; it is just to be taken. If my father wanted sex, it was like a rape to her."

Victor always felt that his father was extremely sadistic; at least, his mother had told him so. "He slapped her around terribly. She was going to divorce him before I was born and she started to work in the hope that she could become economically secure, but he had already impregnated her. She really hated him, and it was important to keep her pregnant in order to keep her with him, even though their lives were miserable. My father often told my mother that he owed her nothing, just food and a roof over her head, and," he murmured sadly, "he told me the same thing."

Before Victor was born, the mother attempted suicide by taking sleeping pills, and the father would not visit her at the hospital. He had been told that before he was born his mother wanted a baby girl. Victor felt that the father was made to take the mother back "because the family threatened to stop talking to him if he would not."

At age nine, he revealed to his father that he and his brother were engaged in kissing and hugging, but did not tell him the full extent of their sexual practices. "My father said it was inconsequential. Had he said it was terrible, I would have told him about the anal intercourse."

Fearful fantasies about the father's death began at age eleven. "If my father dies, when I am twenty-one I will get money. But I am very afraid of his dying. Once I remember playing football and I let go of the ball and it hit his genitals, and he fell over. I burst into tears and ran away, and I never played football again."

At thirteen, he told his father that he was "homosexual." His father said not to worry about it, that he would outgrow it. Around that time, the brother married, and the patient felt sexually jealous. A year or so later, when the brother's wife was in labor, Victor was again "seduced" into anal intercourse by the brother (who proved to have been a sexual

substitute for the father) through his own provocative behavior toward him.

Victor revealed, "Since I was fourteen, I have always been
sexually attracted to my father. Up to two or three years ago,
I'd like that thought. I don't think I could live with his non-
intellectual personality."

After confiding the incestuous acts to his father, Victor
began to flaunt his homosexual involvement with his brother
and his enjoyment of anal intercourse. His brother "pan-
icked" and turned against him. "My father hates him for
seducing me, but I am good to my brother, although I can't
comprehend his being my brother. I do not hate him for
these things. I don't understand why. My father made him
leave the house when he found out."

In the presence of his mother, the patient was always
passive and yielding, except in the matter of his plans for
sexual transformation. In the analytic sessions, she was re-
viled by him. "My mother is two-faced, nauseating. She
seems overly concerned with me now, but she's a shell, too,
and she's dying. She's never satisfied with anything now, but
ceaselessly tries to become socially superior with her country
clubs."

At the age of thirteen the patient developed moderately
severe symptoms of duodenal ulcer and mucous colitis. The
latent signs of the colitis began at the age of seven, simultaneously with his homosexual activity, and represented a
defense against anal penetration and a discharge of his aggression. Colitis attacks continued to be intermittent and
quite severe.

During the course of treatment, the patient revealed that
at the age of seventeen he consciously wished to become pregnant and have a baby. He was engaged in a great deal of
anal intercourse at the time and experienced sensations of
fullness in the anus which persisted beyond the intercourse.
"When men ejaculated into me I wanted very strongly to
have a child by them."

Victor first attempted homosexuality in order to strengthen
his weakened masculine identity through identifying with

a male partner and his penis. But homosexuality was unacceptable to him due to his fears of near-paranoid strength that he would be injured by his male partners. The intensity of his feminine identification pushed him on to try to refute his anatomy, at first by external masquerade through transvestitism (dressing as a female), which did not suffice to resolve his conflict. Finally, he demanded the removal of his external genitalia.

Victor's tenuous hold on reality revealed itself in certain phenomena which occurred upon his attempting to go to sleep. In these states, he would start floating away: he experienced near hallucinations: "I start to spin, and I have to escape faces and figures." He was plagued by a horrifying fantasy, recurrent over the past ten years: "I see a man in a telephone booth with a large penis. It is growing and growing and it fills up the booth and it starts spreading around him and he can't open the door. The man is stuck there. It's growing and it curves and it takes more space, like adding more rope. It looks like it is going to asphyxiate or kill him or strangle him." To Victor, therefore, the penis is a dangerous, growing object which will asphyxiate or destroy him. Psychoanalytically, it represented both the overwhelming maternal body and breast and his attempted merging with the breast and the body of the mother, and the threat of personal annihilation implicit in this. These conclusions were verified by analysis of his dream material. It was also the father's tremendous phallus as seen by the infant which can asphyxiate the child through anal penetration or oral incorporation. The telephone booth symbolized his attempt to find safety within the maternal body, but this enclosure into which he put himself through regression became an inescapable trap and threat to his survival. The psychoanalysis of this fantasy revealed a crucial conflict. He dared not become a female (merge and join with the mother) nor did he dare to become a "male" (engaging in homosexual activities, which would lend temporary feelings of masculinity by identifying with the male partner and his penis). In the latter event he would be killed by the penis itself (the huge phallus of the father).

It became apparent that his desire for sexual transformation was nevertheless necessary to defend himself against paranoid fears of aggression. "I will sacrifice everything to change. If you have a vagina, you can control people, you can control them sexually. The idea fascinates me and to use this vagina fascinates me. I think I'm scared of anal intercourse. I could have intercourse with men with a vagina and I would not be harmed physiologically, but I already have been harmed through anal intercourse with men. I remember the first time my brother did it to me. He said he'd stay home to see that nothing happened to me afterward, but I got a colitis attack after my first intercourse with him. My nervous rectum is due to my having anal intercourse."

Because of my patient's primary feminine identification, he wished to replace the mother in sexual relations with the father. This he gratified in a substitutive way, not only in homosexual relations, but also in the creation of a substitute father, the plaster-of-Paris Man.

Around the age of fourteen, he would masturbate with pictures of his father in his mind. To heighten fulfillment and satisfaction, he devised a mannequin and preserved it until he was eighteen. "When I got hold of this plaster-of-Paris mannequin, I was perfectly happy. I'd take my father's robe and put it around him. I loved my father's hands, and I made a plaster-of-Paris cast of them and attached them to the sleeves of the bathrobe and would tie the hands around my body. It's a lost passion. I had one finger of the plaster hand lifted. I immersed it in paraffin so it would be softer and fleshlike. I had gigantic pillows for his body and I would put this complete plaster-of-Paris man in bed with me. I liked to lay him beside me and have his arms around me and his hands on my penis or the lifted finger inside my anus. Sometimes I would use a sausage for this purpose while the plaster-of-Paris man was embracing me. One day I had him in the closet and the maid opened the door and she was terrified. I had put a hook on him and hung him on the back of the closet door."

His dreams continually portrayed his conflict. They represented his fear and dread of the surgery which he consciously and ardently desired, but unconsciously feared. One of the dreams is described here:

"A gigantic building, empty, built of white stucco but kind of old. There were no stairs, three levels. I was on the third floor with no steps. I think I am being chased or I'm afraid, and then I remember jumping down. I was embarrassed for people to see me, only half of my legs were shaven. From my knees down, hair was present. Also on my face, it was like I hadn't shaved for six months. I was shocked when I kept getting views of my unshaven legs, of what they looked like to others. In this dream, I'm also an observer. I only see what Victor sees, however. I see one-half and one-half, similar to when I dress as Valerie. When I look into the mirror now I see Valerie's eyes; the rest is me, Victor. It's me looking at somebody else. It was like a big architect's studio. It was like the whole building was covered except for the doors. If you opened the doors there'd be nothing inside and you couldn't see anything. I think I have a fear of death because I don't think, somehow, in the end, I may live through this. Maybe it's vagina I'm looking at. Could be, because there are some mahogany doors and my nipples are now like the color of these doors. There is a draping around, a kind of draping which one finds in an operation. I was thinking of the operation yesterday and I started shivering. The transsexual doctor tells me how calm people are, having the operation. I remembered that and then I stopped shivering."

In the patient's operation dream, one could see the intense anxiety over the creation of a vagina, a frightening, empty place where his penis used to be; the fear of death in surgery; the fear of psychotic disintegration upon being given an anesthetic with its alteration of consciousness and spatial relationship; the split betwen the unconscious image of self —only Valerie's eyes remain—and his actual male anatomical

self has disappeared. The patient is obviously terrified of
the surgery which he so adamantly insists upon.

Other dreams and fantasies revealed that in his unconscious, Victor-Valerie saw his father as wanting him to have
the surgery and he himself harbored the wish to supplant
the mother in the father's affections. His father promises him
in other dreams that he will permit him to "change" sex so
that they may have sexual intercourse together. His reaction
to the possibility of such a fulfillment was ambivalent and
he would weep in desperation. The basic motivation for
sexual transformation in many of his dreams was herein
revealed: in replacing the mother, he would fulfill his primary feminine identification (becoming the mother) and
thereby attain the father's love and triumph over the mother.

Shortly after abruptly terminating treatment with me at
the age of twenty-one, the patient was seen in further consultation regarding the advisability of surgery by Dr. Harold
Rosen, of the University of Maryland School of Medicine,
who conducted a hypnotic session with him. Dr. Rosen
knew nothing of my views at that time and had not yet
received any report of his therapy from me. Part of his independent investigation is here quoted from a personal
communication.

> While this patient was talking about his place of work,
> stating that he had already told his boss that he was going
> to live completely like a woman, get a job as a woman, he
> was hypnotized by passing his conscious awareness of this.
> Immediately upon hypnotic induction, he started to breathe
> more and more deeply, started raising his left hand, and
> kept it partly turned with the index finger pointed toward
> the ceiling and then rose from the chair and started to walk
> toward the couch. Only by the second step did he develop
> *flexibilitas cerea* (waxy flexibility as seen in catatonic schizo-
> phrenia). Movements were so slow as to make it take him
> almost ten minutes to reach the couch. He raised his right
> leg—in order, it seemed to me, to swing partly around and
> sit down or lie down—but then retained the partly raised
> position, remaining catatonic during the next fifteen to

twenty minutes. He was mute. A suggestion was then given him; he could, he was told, if it did not provoke too much anxiety, tell me what he was thinking or picturing much the same way that a television newscaster discusses the pictures flashed on the television screen.

The suggestion was effective. He spoke very slowly—but he spoke. He was thinking of the operation he had had two years ago. (As he continued, it turned out that he had *progressed three years in the future.*) He had taken six months to have his hair electrolyzed, to get a complete wardrobe, to give up his present job and get another job as a woman, to move, to take the name Valerie instead of Victor, to black out his complete previous life and to become established completely as a—he did not use the word "woman" —"girl." He had not let anyone know where he was living or where he was working. For an additional six months he had lived completely as a woman. He then—this therefore was after a year—had had the operation here at Johns Hopkins and had gone back to New York to his job as a woman, hoping to meet someone who would marry him so he could become a housewife and raise an (adopted) family. Instead, he was jeered at and despised, and called a "Lesbian" or a "dike" just as he had been called this before he had undergone the surgery.

But worse still, his father had employed a detective, had located him, had forced himself upon him, and had begun having (heterosexual) relations with him against his will. There was no way he could stop his father. But he had struggled so much when his father's penis got into his vagina that he had damaged it—his father's organ—and made it atrophied (his phrase was "wither off"), which is what he wanted to do anyhow every time he heard that his father had been having relations with his mother three times a week throughout their marriage. But his father somehow managed to regrow a penis, a bigger one than before, and for the last year, three times a week, they would be having anal intercourse in just about the same way as between the ages of seven and fourteen his brother had had anal intercourse with him.

This was all apparently background material. To repeat: He had projected himself into the future three years after getting the surgery he is now requesting. What he had been thinking and planning (during the catatonic period in my office) was how to kill his father. He would get some drug and sprinkle it on his food, but not quite enough to put him completely to sleep, so that when he is half-asleep or so he could still get him sexually aroused to the point of having a big erection—but because of the drug his father would be much too sleepy to have the strength to do anything about it. He would cut it off. His first thought was that of pushing it down his father's throat so that his father would choke to death with it. But what he was doing instead was to picture sewing it on himself and changing his vagina back into male organs.

How long would he have to stop taking estrogen and instead be taking testosterone to be able to use it? Should he start using it on his brother and work up to his father or should he start using it on his father without practicing on his brother?

After the hypnotic trance, Dr. Rosen adds, "The patient discussed the fact that up to the present he had not been able to feel that he is either a male or a female. He is anatomically a male now taking estrogen but tells people he is a female on testosterone. Does this mean he cannot tell which way he is heading toward establishing a male or a female identity?"

The remarkable hypnotic session conducted by Dr. Rosen confirmed my findings that, beneath what has been referred to by proponents of surgery as simply "a female psyche wrapped in a male body," there existed a full-blown paranoid schizophrenic psychosis with catatonic elements. The catatonic position while in the hypnotic trance with uplifted finger is a remarkable replication of the plaster-of-Paris Man (his father, himself) from whom he wished to acquire love and masculinity in late adolescence. The insoluble dilemma of the transsexual is present: on the one hand, he wishes to be a woman replacing his mother and becoming the mother, which would bring about his being raped by the father and allow a vengeful retaliation on his part against the father and brother; on the other hand, the wish to be a man induces great guilt as it is tantamount to castrating and murdering his father. In his homosexuality, there is a wish to be like the father; therefore, the father's destruction is his own destruction. Consequently, both positions—female and male—are unbearable.

Behind Victor-Valerie's conscious wish to remove his penis and acquire a vagina surgically and therefore permanently lies another wish: to change his body to female for a while and then change it back again to male. Having withered the penis of the father through intercourse (weakened him), he then appropriates the regrown erect and enormous paternal penis, thereby capturing his long-lost masculinity. The method by which this would be accomplished is by the sexual-transformation procedure—i.e., by getting rid of his own penis he entices the father to intercourse; the intercourse leads to the disarming of his father by acquiring the father's penis; he has the father in his power; in this position, he has the father's penis and now "magically" can become a man.

The transsexual procedure working one way, in the unconscious of the patient, can certainly work in the opposite direction. Through the omnipotence of his thought, he not only can be turned into a woman but also he can be turned back into a man—hopefully, not the false, dead, plaster-of-Paris man, the father who did not love him except in effigy.

# Chapter 10

# FUTURE SEX

## Drugs, Electrodes, and the Genital Bypass

*With the advance of organic chemistry, the manufacture of the most refined substances for producing sexual gratification is as surely only a matter of time, and it is easy to prophesy that in the future of our race this mode of gratification will play a part as yet incalculable.*
          —SANDOR RADO: "Narcotic Bondage" (1957)

Man pursues goals—his own prosperity and the welfare of those he loves and cares for. The pursuit requires effort and performance. Expending effort and energy is an essential "painful" prerequisite toward his objective. The striving necessary for man to sustain his pursuits is promoted by the knowledge of the forthcoming reward of pleasure and the satisfaction he will experience upon successful fulfillment of his task. The striving must be real in order for the reward to be real—no gains without effort and energy expended.

Narcotic drugs have the effect of producing a deceptive sense of achievement tantamount to elation, a false sense of triumph and accomplishment. Tragically, they cause both a psychological craving of the mind and a physiological "craving" of the cell.

The magic of narcotic drugs lies in their biochemical action on the brain, in bypassing prerequisite adaptive efforts and performance. They lift one, as if by magic, from a state of pain to a state of pleasure. The reaction of the self to such an immediate and instantaneous change is a feeling of all-power, almightiness, in which the ego expands, problems vanish, and a conviction of invulnerability suffuses the organism. Elation may become so prominent that it may entirely replace or substitute the need for sexual orgasm, thereby resulting in the bypassing of genital pleasure (*the genital bypass*).

This is super-pleasure—super-intense pleasure without effort. In every way it is subversive to man's enlightened self-interest. It seduces the individual to abandon the pain-pleasure principle of reality based on delayed reward and to regress to the level of instant—and illusory—gratification without effort.

Therefore, why should anyone expend effort in work, play, or achievement? In effect, one thus returns to living on the basis of simply the contact receptors, the hedonic level of the onion brain (see Chapter 1). At that point man is, in a sense, fully dehumanized like the amoeba.

Whether taking narcotic drugs or wearing a chest console attached to centers in his brain, the individual is engaging in the self-stimulation comparable to Dr. James Olds's electrode-implanted animals.[121] It is known that if the pharmacological and/or electrical stimulation of the pleasure centers is continued, momentous changes in both psyche and soma occur. The greatest alterations are those in the sexual sphere. Rado has warned: "Erotic gratification by means of drugs is a violent attack on our biological sexual organization, a bold forward movement of our 'alloplastic' civilization. . . ." For example, when morphine is injected, the "whole peripheral sexual apparatus if left on one side as in a 'short circuit,' and the exciting stimuli are enabled to operate directly on the central organ."[125]

In time one may therefore not need affectionate relatedness to another person—or even need another person at all—for sexual gratification. Radical sexualists may be outstripped by the laboratory. Science will do them one better: not only will it be all right to have sex with anyone at any time, providing the state permits it, but no union of male and female genitals will be involved; simply a drug or electrode will suffice.

By the year 2000 people will be able to wear chest consoles with tin levers wired to the brain's pleasure centers.[77] Leon Kass envisages a world in which man pursues only artificially induced sensation, a world in which the arts have died, books are no longer read, and human beings do not even bother to think or to govern themselves.[86] A physicist, John Taylor, predicts a world in which there is "so much fun" that people will want to give up practically all non-sexual activities;[170] this seems a distinct possibility. The claim has already been made that there are discoveries which show that there are "things better than sex."

In the early 1950s, physiological experiments on animals led to the discovery of "pleasure centers" in the brain. Electrical stimulation of these centers gave the animal a special pleasure reward, similar to the super-pleasure induced biochemically by narcotic drugs.

In 1956, James Olds, using the Skinner method, implanted animals with electrodes. They were put in a "do-it-yourself situation," so that by pressing a lever they were able to stimulate their own brain.

> The animals seemed to experience the strongest reward or pleasure from stimulation of areas of the hypothalamus and certain mid-brain nuclei-regions which Hess and others had found to be centers for control of digestive, sexual, excretory and similar processes. Animals with electrodes in these areas would stimulate themselves from 500 to 5,000 times per hour.
>
> Electric stimulation in some of these regions actually appeared to be far more rewarding to the animals than an ordinary satisfier such as food. . . . Indeed a hungry animal often ignored available food in favor of the pleasure of

stimulating itself electrically. Some rats with electrodes in these places stimulated their brains more than 2,000 times per hour for 24 consecutive hours.[121]

Any drug which produces an effortless elation, feelings of grandeur, and removal of pain and suffering as if by magic is potentially a corrupter of the pleasure-pain self-regulation apparatus. It is an agent in the aphanisis of sex, if not the aphanisis of mankind. This is true of drugs from the mildest to the strongest, from marijuana to LSD and morphine, and to others as yet only imagined in the laboratory.

For example, let us examine in this context the most widely used and most controversial substance, marijuana. In relatively small doses it produces an objective alteration of time-and-space perception. It has a relatively mild action on the pleasure centers of the brain compared to the opiates. It increases sexual desire, when already present, and seems to prolong orgastic time. But at higher doses there comes a "dulling of attention, fragmentation of thought, impaired immediate memory, an altered sense of identity, exaggerated laughter, and an increased suggestibility. Other less common effects are dizziness, a feeling of lightness, nausea, and hunger. As doses higher than the typical social dose are consumed, more pronounced thought distortions may occur, including a disrupted sense of one's own body, a sense of personal unreality, visual distortions, and sometimes hallucinations and paranoid thinking."[106]

But does marijuana cause a corruption of the hedonic self-regulatory apparatus? In small, infrequent doses, no. It can work as a harmless enhancement to pleasurable stimuli. Frequent heavy use, however, is correlated with a loss of interest in goals and with the development of lethargy. The mechanism for this end result is embodied implicitly in the super-pleasure concept.

Does marijuana expand consciousness and improve lovemaking, enhance relatedness to another person? Ultimately, no. Interviews conducted by Dr. L. J. West, of the University of California School of Medicine, revealed the corruption of the self through super-pleasure.[181] He reports that the continuous use of marijuana results in apathy, loss of effectiveness, and a diminished capacity or willingness to carry out complex long-term plans. The ability to tolerate frustration, concentrate for long periods, follow routines, or successfully master new material is also decreased. Verbal facility is often impaired, both in writing and in speaking. For many students a slow progressive change from conforming, achievement-oriented behavior to a state of careless drifting has followed the use of significant amounts of marijuana over a period of time. But, the report notes, the *occasional* user should be separated from the *habitual*.[181]

West's interviews were conducted with users in the Haight-Ashbury area of San Francisco from the fall of 1966 to January, 1968. His findings of generalized inhibition must certainly reflect itself in a long-range sexual apathy and frustration. This symptom tends to become generalized. If one is apathetic in work and achievement in the group-membership area, one is ultimately apathetic in the sexual.

Marijuana is the least potent of the elatent drugs, surely not a villain if not abused.[58, 59, 80] Heroin and the true narcotics, at the opposite end of the spectrum, quickly and effectively produce a devastation threatening survival. One can only speculate what man with his increasingly sophisticated technology will concoct to bypass and "surpass" genital functioning.

As Rado says, "the crux of the matter is, that it is the pharmacogenic pleasure effect which discharges the libidinal tension associated with . . . fantasies. . . . The genital apparatus with its extensive auxilliary ramifications in the erotogenic zones falls into desuetude and is overtaken by a sort of mental atrophy of disuse. The fire of life is gradually extinguished at that point where it should glow most intensely according to nature and is kindled at a site contrary to nature."[125]

Drugs of all kinds can too easily deaden and distort those elusive and capricious aspects of personality which we dare attempt to stimulate, manipulate or control.

## *The New Asexual Reproduction: Clonal Man*

*The impact of the new birth technology may strike home on earth, splintering our traditional notions of sexuality, motherhood, love, child-rearing and education. Discussions about the future of the family that deal only with the Pill overlook the biological witches' brew now seething in the laboratories. The moral and emotional choices that will confront us in the coming decades are mind-staggering. . . . In short, it is safe to say that, unless specific countermeasures are taken, if something can be done, someone, somewhere, will do it. The nature of what can and will be done exceeds anything that man is as yet psychologically or morally prepared to live with.*

—ALVIN TOFFLER: *Future Shock*

Man is now in a position—through the complex science of genetic engineering—to be able eventually to abandon sexual reproduction altogether, assuming that current experimentation by microbial geneticists continues successfully.[28, 108, 131, 133] A stage of human development will come to an end.

Evolutionary history dates back two and a half billion years, but man was "born" only thirty-five thousand years ago—a brief interval on the evolutionary time scale. He may never be allowed the luxury of undergoing further phylogenetic development, thereby enhancing or improving the species. We will have come full circle: from asexual reproduction of one-celled animal life (fission, meiosis), evolution arrived at sexual reproduction (mitosis). The genetic engineers are making it possible for man to revert to asexual reproduction, albeit a new and modern form, asexual in that reproduction may take place without sexual desire and without a sexual act between man and women. The xeroxed copies of individuals produced by cloning (from the Greek word for "throng") will become the analogue to the carbon copies of splitting by fission. This event opens up the possibility that sexual intercourse between two individuals who love each other—lovemaking, which is the humanizer of life—may be entirely eliminated. The triumphal cry is that for the first time in all time a living creature understands its origin and can undertake to design its future.[142]

Laboratory reproduction became a viable scientific possibility when Dr. J. B. Gurdon, of Oxford University, took an unfertilized egg cell from an African clawed frog, destroyed its nucleus by ultraviolet radiation, and replaced it with the nucleus of an intestinal cell from a tadpole of the same species. This was an epoch-making procedure. The egg, discovering that it had a full set of chromosomes, instead of the half set found in unfertilized eggs, responded by beginning to divide as if it had been normally fertilized. The result was a tadpole that was the genetic twin of the tadpole that provided the nucleus. This was proof of what geneticists have long known: all of the genetic information necessary to produce an organism is coded into the nucleus of every cell in that organism.

It is possible now to insert an adult human diploid nucleus into a human egg whose maternal genetic material has previously been removed. Experimenters in England are already working out the conditions for routine test-tube conception —of human eggs. They have developed many embryos to the eight-cell and a few more into blastocytes, the stage where successful implantation into a human uterus has recently been achieved. This accomplishment is of particular value and significance for those women who until now could not become pregnant due to blocked oviducts which prevent passage of the egg into the uterus. The implantation of the fertilized egg directly into the uterus took place in England in late 1973 and now makes childbearing a possibility in such cases, as attested to by the delivery of several normal healthy babies in the spring of 1974. (*Medical World News*, August 9, 1974).

This achievement also opens up the possibility of hiring unrelated surrogate mothers to carry a given baby to term. James D. Watson, the Nobel laureate, believes there is absolutely no reason why the blastocyte needs to be implanted in the same woman from whom the preovulatory eggs were obtained.[179] It is predicted that women who do not want the discomfort of pregnancy would seek this different form of motherhood. In fairness to Watson, it should be noted that he is "worried" about the misuse of these discoveries by an inhuman totalitarian government while he points out that through such genetic manipulation one may eradicate a number of genetic diseases.

The exponents of this form of the new asexual reproduction point to the benefits for mankind from genetic engineering. For example, manipulation of an embryo during gestation may completely change its physical characteristics. We will have an alternative to natural human reproduction: the implantation of a fertilized ovum into the womb of a "host" mother or into an artificial womb in a laboratory. There is a possibility of creating children with only one parent; biological duplicates of a single parent are a definite possibility.

Switching a fertilized ovum from the womb of a woman after she has conceived and then implanting it in the uterus of another woman who would ultimately give birth could easily be arranged. The proxy mother would be only a temporary host. But why stop there? Technology could go a step further and simply eliminate the process of pregnancy and childbirth altogether.[61, 129]

A human embryo can be removed from the uterus and placed in an artificial womb, although the removal of waste products has been a stumbling block. Carbon copies of a human being already in existence resulting from a process much more revolutionary than the merging of sperm and egg in a test tube are a major next step. Clonal man has nearly arrived: fertilized in a test tube without sexual relations and then grown in an artificial womb in a factory-laboratory.

A woman who presents three sons and two daughters as "her children" may be doing so by every biological rule but one—that she has never been pregnant. On five occasions sex cells from her body and her husband's were implanted in the wombs of proxy mothers who were paid to carry each fetus and to give it birth.

Architects of the new biological revolution happily predict that test-tube growth using an artificial placenta (ecto-genesis) will make natural pregnancy an anachronism. The uterus in time may become appendixlike, though the ovaries will be as necessary as ever. At the age of twenty, each woman will be able to choose to be superovulated and her eggs collected and frozen because babies conceived by younger women are not as likely to suffer from mongolism or other birth defects. Women who wish to "put up" with the old style of sexual reproduction and all that it implies will be permitted to do so by those in authority, but this will be a throwback and increasingly rare as the public-health "ad-vantages" of the artificial womb become obvious. These are what are currently touted as benefits to mankind.

Most startling of all will be the clonal type of man himself. The development of simple techniques for fusing animal cells has raised the strong possibility that further refinements of the cell-fusion method would allow the routine introduc-tion of human diploid nuclei into *enucleated* human eggs. "Activation of such eggs to divide, to become blastocytes, followed by implantation into suitable uteri, should lead to the development of healthy fetuses, and subsequently nor-mal-appearing babies. The growing up to adulthood of these first clonal humans would be a very startling event."[170] For example, a prominent rock singer may have skin tissue scraped from his arm, and nine months later three hundred babies will emerge from a factory which contains an equal number of artificial wombs. These offspring will be genetic carbon copies of the singer.

Thus man will be able to clone or asexually reproduce himself, creating thousands of virtually identical twins from a test-tube full of cells, carried through gestation by donor mothers or hatched in an artificial womb. Using such a tech-nique, a woman in the future might have a child cloned from one of her own cells. The child would inherit all of its mother's characteristics, including, of course, her sex. Many scientists,[140] for example, embryologist Robert T. Francoeur,[129] abhor the mere idea of cloning. They feel it is one of the things that men should never do, this xeroxing of people. Cloning itself would threaten the basic social unit, the family.

Artificial inovulation (the prenatal adoption of someone else's fertilized egg), women hiring mercenaries to bear their children, and babies born in hatcheries would create serious psychological difficulties, a fact apparent even to those without psychological training. There is a wholesale violation of spiritual and physical faithfulness between husband and wife, parent and child, implicit in all of these innovations. It is quite possible that the artificial womb is the instrument which will produce nothing but psychological monsters, due to the lack of intrauterine development in the mother and the subsequent loss of care of the young by the parents. The family will disappear.

In my opinion, these developments will have disastrous effects on the mind and body of everyone, men no less than women. Access to an artificial womb goes against the deepest instinct provided by nature. Should a woman "having a baby" via the artificial womb take estrogens orally? Women will be alienated from their children, causing further distance during the crucial beginning of life. The baby's intrauterine environment is absolutely essential for its subsequent healthy psychological development. It is imperative for the mother to carry the child within herself and for the child to be carried within the mother. By cheating life we will be raising ultimate questions that we are not prepared to answer.

The artificial womb will not, in fact, "create" life, for the materials which contain all the factors for differentiation, growth, and genetic coding—the egg and the sperm—cannot be fabricated. They will be given another environment in which to work out their processes. But sexual reproduction will not be necessary; sexual intercourse and pleasure, separated from each other and from childbearing and childbirth, may lose their vital meaning. Sexual intercourse, when it occurs, will have a different place in the life of man.

Dr. Leon Kass of the National Academy of Sciences asks, "Is there not some wisdom in the mystery of nature that joins the pleasure of sex, the communication of love, and the desire for children in the very activity by which we continue the chain of human existence; is not human procreation, if properly understood and practiced, itself a humanizing experience? . . . Destruction of the family unit would throw us, even more than we are now, on the mercy of an impersonal, lonely present."[86] Sir McFarland Burset, microbiologist and another Nobel Laureate, agrees that what we face is an "appalling catastrophe." It could be "equally genocidal" as the production of the nuclear bomb.[22]

Those scientists encouraging genetic experimentation are putting their faith in man's rational power, but others fear a terrifying, uncontrollable, Huxleyian nightmare. To psychoanalysts, furthering these genetic experiments is to write an end to man's highest aspirations and goals. Separating sex from love, adults from children, parents from the care of their young plunges mankind into the ultimate psychological catastrophe with only technological and impersonal skills to guide it. Man, as the beast of pride, unhampered by honor, joy, tenderness, goodwill, would have no safeguards against reverting to cruelty, lust, desire for power and primordial omnipotence.

The infant will not have parents who are responsible for its fecundation, birth and delivery, care and growth. Sex may well be practiced solely for the release of instinctual pressures which will periodically build up and need expression. This could be facilitated either through the use of machines or impersonally through the use of sexual partners who are strangers to their mates. Tenderness, affectivity, love, joy, and other social emotions would not play a central part in man's growth and development. Could one then still experience love? It is unlikely, as the emotions of love and joy are learned and arise out of the prolonged period of dependency that a child and adolescent experience.

The psychological effects of extrauterine conception and "birth" through the artificial womb are terrifying. For the child, mother, father, and siblings, tremendous changes would take place. Ordinarily, the first two years of life, in which the child is brought up by the mother, are crucial to the development of mental illness or mental health. The revised relationship between the mother and father would have devastating effects on any offspring throughout life, from infancy to senescence. A new type of creature, a new form of man, may well evolve.

Can the work on human embryos be outlawed? Shouldn't it be? At what point are scientists responsible for their discoveries and their effect on the future of mankind? This is a crucial point in man's history: a time when the interrelationship of responsibility between science, technology, and humanity must be reevaluated.

Yale physiologist José Delgado feels that man should press full speed ahead in these endeavors, as he cannot wait for natural selection to change him; the process is much too slow. Delgado likens the human animal to the dinosaur: insufficiently intelligent to adapt to its changing environment. He is oversimplifying the problem when he states that men are simply the "victims of emotional anachronisms, of internal drives essential to survival in a primitive past, but undesirable in a civilized state."[32] Delgado believes man, by these new efforts, can sharpen his intellect and curb his aboriginal urges, as if this were at all possible in this manner.

To the psychoanalyst, the "onion brain" (see Chapter 1) will still have to be taken into account; only total destruction of ovum and sperm can eradicate man's primordial past. The onion brain and its collective primordial "inhabitants"—the hedonic one-celled creature, the beast of prey, the beast of brute emotion, the beast of pride (man)—reside within every individual and cannot be eradicated through genetic engineering.

# EPILOGUE

My purpose throughout this book has been not only to analyze current and emerging sexual practices but also to speculate as to their probable consequences. In their investigative and healing aims, psychoanalysts continually ask three major questions: "What is the meaning of an event or piece of behavior or symptom?" (cause-searching), "Where did it come from?" (end-relating, means to ends), and "What can be done to correct things?" It is within such a framework that this material has been presented.

Unlike the lower species, man, in his unique ability to *become* the "beast of pride," holds in his hands at this very moment the possibilities of the nightmarish future described by Anderson in the Introduction. He *also* holds the power to channel all his unique capacities into directions that lead to his ultimate enrichment, happiness, and advancement. The choice is his.

The time has come for man to face the conditions he has created for himself in recent years, face them and deal with them. He must learn to regard objectively a false "freedom" which has been touted as the panacea to all the ills of the human condition. This "freedom" from responsibility, from the constraints of tradition and family life is but a topsy-turvy attempt to mitigate the natural difficulties of a functioning, feeling human being by simply throwing everything we regard as important in life upside down—as if to say, "If family doesn't work, let's try no-family," "If heterosexuality isn't satisfying, let's try homosexuality," "If tradition doesn't work, let's try anti-tradition," "If you don't like what sex you are, try the opposite"—in other words, let's unthinkingly turn the world on its head, for we can do anything we like; this is the voice of the beast of pride. The voice is still small, but it tries to rise to a roar. There is still time for the voice of reason to prevail.

Man must and shall rediscover the pleasure of what takes effort. He will again heed his own conscience and good sense. He will reaffirm what he has always known, that to be a human creature is the most difficult and most responsible and most rewarding condition in the world, that the pleasures and responsibilities of sexuality—as of family and of society—are part of the same long and varied continuum. Man will affirm his individual identity and with it his social, sexual, and cultural identity as the highest and most mysterious of creatures. He will realize that there is no freedom without dignity, no freedom without identity.

# REFERENCES

1. Alexander, Franz. *Our Age of Unreason: A Study of the Irrational Forces in Social Life.* N.Y.: Lippincott, 1951.
2. Alexander, Franz. *The Western Mind in Transition.* N.Y.: Random House, 1960.
3. Anderson, Robert. *Solitaire, Double Solitaire.* N.Y.: Play Service Inc., 1971.
4. Angel, Klaus. "A Psychoanalyst Suggests—No Marijuana for Adolescents." *N.Y. Times Magazine,* Nov. 30, 1969, pp. 170–178.
5. Arlow, J. A. *The Legacy of Sigmund Freud.* N.Y.: International Universities Press, 1956.
6. Asimov, Isaac, quoted in "Grave New World." *Saturday Review.* April 8, 1972, p. 27.
7. Bartell, Gilbert D. *Group Sex.* N.Y.: Peter H. Wyden, 1971.
8. Benedek, T. *Psychosexual Functions in Women.* N.Y.: Ronald Press, 1952.
9. Benjamin, H. *The Transsexual Phenomenon.* N.Y.: Julian Press, 1966.
10. Bergler, E. *Selected Papers of Edmund Bergler.* N.Y.: Grune & Stratton, 1969.
11. Bergler, E. *Counterfeit Sex.* N.Y.: Grune & Stratton, 1951.
12. Bergler, E., and Kroger, W. *Kinsey's Myth of Female Sexuality: The Medical Facts.* N.Y.: Grune & Stratton, 1954.
13. Bergler, E. *1000 Homosexuals: Conspiracy of Silence on Curing and Deglamorizing Homosexuality.* Paterson, N.J.: Pageant Books, 1959.
14. Bieber, I., et al. *Homosexuality.* N.Y.: Basic Books, 1962.
15. Blaine, Graham B., and Carmen, Lida R. "Causal Factors in Suicidal Attempts by Male and Female College Students." *Amer. J. Psychiatry.* 125:6, Dec. 1968, pp. 834–838.
16. Blos, P. *On Adolescence.* N.Y.: Free Press, 1961.

17. Blumenthal, R. "Communes and Communards." *N.Y. Times Magazine,* Dec. 1, 1968.

18. Bonaparte, M. *Female Sexuality.* N.Y.: International Universities Press, 1953.

19. Bonaparte, M., Freud, A., and Kris, E. *The Origins of Psycho-Analysis: Letters of Wilhelm Fliess* (Tr. E. Mosbacher & J. Strachey). N.Y.: Basic Books, 1954.

20. Brierly, Marjorie. "Specific Determinants in Feminine Development." *Int. J. Psychoanal.* 17:163–180, 1935.

21. Bunney, William E., Leff, Melitta J., and Roatch, John F. "Environmental Factors Preceding the Onset of Severe Depressions." U.S. Dept. of Health, Education, and Welfare, National Institutes of Health, NIH-53249.

22. Burset, McFarland, quoted in "The Future of Genetic Engineering." *Medical Tribune.* June 15, 1970.

23. Bychowski, G. "The Ego of Homosexuals." *Int. J. Psychoanal.* 26:114–127, 1945.

24. Cannon, W. B. *Bodily Changes in Pain, Hunger, Fear and Rage.* N.Y.: Appleton-Century, 1934.

25. Churchill, Wainwright. *Homosexual Behavior Among Males: A Cross-Cultural and Cross-Species Investigation.* N.Y.: Hawthorn, 1967.

26. Comfort, Alexander. "Sexuality in a Zero Growth Society." Center for the Study of Democratic Institutions Report. Dec., 1972. pp. 12–14.

27. Comfort, Alexander. *The Joy of Sex.* N.Y.: Simon & Schuster, 1972.

28. "Controversial Test-Tube Conceptions." *Medical World News.* Vol. 10, no. 14, April 4, 1969. pp. 26–32.

29. Cooper, David. *The Death of the Family.* N.Y.: Pantheon, 1970.

30. Crowley, Mark. *The Boys in the Band.* N.Y.: Dell, 1969.

31. Decter, Midge. *The New Chastity and Other Arguments Against Women's Liberation.* N.Y.: Coward, McCann & Geoghegan, 1972.

32. Delgado, José, quoted in "The Mind: From Memory Pills to Electronic Pleasures Beyond Sex." *Time.* April 19, 1971, p. 45.

33. Deutsch, H. "On Female Homosexuality." *Psychoanal. Quart.* 1:484–510, 1932.

34. Deutsch, H. *The Psychology of Women,* vol. I & II. N.Y.: Grune & Stratton, 1944.

35. Deutsch, H. *A Psychoanalytic Study of the Myth of Dionysus and Apollo: Two Variants of the Son-Mother Relationship.* N.Y.: International Universities Press, 1969.

36. Ellis, Albert. *Homosexuality, Its Causes and Cure.* N.Y.: Lyle Stuart, 1965.

37. Fenichel, O. *The Psychoanalytic Theory of Neurosis.* N.Y.: Norton, 1945, pp. 340–343.

38. Ford, C. S., and Beach, F. A. *Patterns of Sexual Behavior.* N.Y.: Harper-Hoeber, 1951.

39. Fowles, John. *The Collector.* Boston: Little, Brown, 1963.

40. Freud, A. "Some Clinical Remarks Concerning the Treatment of Cases of Male Homosexuality" (summary of presentation before the International Psychoanalytical Congress, Zurich, 1949) *Int. J. Psychoanal.* 30: 195, 1949.

41. Freud, S. *The Complete Psychological Works of Sigmund Freud,* vols. 1–23. Standard Edition. London: Hogarth Press, 1953–1964.

42. Freud, S. "Three Essays on the Theory of Sexuality" (1905). *Complete Psychological Works,* vol. 7, pp. 125–244.

43. Freud, S. "Five Lectures on Psychoanalysis" (1910). *Complete Psychological Works,* vol. 11, pp. 3–56.

44. Freud, S. "Totem and Taboo" (1912). *Complete Psychological Works,* vol. 13, pp. 1–162.

45. Freud, S. "Psychogenesis of a Case of Homosexuality in a Woman" (1920). *Complete Psychological Works,* vol. 18, pp. 145–175.

46. Freud, S. "The Sexual Life of Human Beings" (1920). Introductory Lectures on Psychoanalysis, Lecture 20. *Complete Psychological Works,* vol. 16, pp. 303–320.

47. Freud, S. "Civilization and Its Discontents" (1929). *Complete Psychological Works,* vol. 21 pp. 59–64.

48. Freud, S. "An Outline of Psychoanalysis" (1940). *Complete Psychological Works,* vol. 23, pp. 144–205.

49. Freud, S. "The Neuroses: Traumas. The Unconscious," in *A General Introduction to Psychoanalysis.* N.Y.: Garden City Publishing Co., 1943, p. 252.

50. Friedan, Betty. Quoted in article by Enid Nemy, *N.Y. Times Magazine,* Oct. 2, 1972.

51. Gadpaille, Warren J. "Homosexual Activity and Homosexuality in Adolescence," in Masserman, J. H., *Dynamics of Deviant Sexuality.* N.Y.: Grune & Stratton, 1969, pp. 60–71.

52. Galdston, Iago, editor. *Freud and Contemporary Culture.* N.Y.: International Universities Press, 1957.

53. Gant, Herbert M. "Controversy Rages Over Transsexual Operations." *Psychiat. News.* Aug. 1969, p. 14.

54. Gebhard, Paul H., Gagnon, John H., Pomeroy, W. B., and Christenson, C. V. *Sex Offenders.* N.Y.: Harper & Row, 1965.

55. Gerassi, J. *The Boys of Boise.* N.Y.: Macmillan, 1966.

56. Glover, E. *The Roots of Crime: Selected Papers on Psychoanalysis,* vol. 2. London: The Imago Publishing Co., Ltd., 1960.

57. Golding, S. *The Inevitability of Patriarchy.* N.Y.: Morrow, 1973.

58. Goode, Erich, editor. *Marihuana.* N.Y.: Atherton, 1969.

59. Goode, Erich. "Turning on for Fun." *N.Y. Times.* Op-Ed page, Jan. 9, 1971.

60. Greer, Germaine. *The Female Eunuch.* N.Y.: McGraw-Hill, 1970.

61. Grossman, Edward. "The Obsolescent Mother." *Atlantic Monthly.* 1971, pp. 39–50.

62. "Group Sex: Its Impact on Marriage and Mental Health.: *Frontiers of Clinical Psychiatry.* Vol. 7, no. 11, June 1, 1970, pp. 1–11.

63. Hamill, Pete. *N.Y. Post.* July 13, 1970.

64. Hatterer, Lawrence J. *Changing Homosexuality in the Male.* N.Y.: McGraw-Hill, 1970.

65. Hendin, Herbert. *Suicide and Scandinavia: A Psychoanalytic Study of Culture and Character.* N.Y.: Grune & Stratton, 1964.

66. Henry, G. W. *Sex Variants: A Study of Homosexual Patterns.* N.Y.: Hoeber, 1941.

67. Highet, Gilbert. *The Art of Teaching.* N.Y.: Knopf, 1950.

68. Hoffman, Martin. *The Gay World.* N.Y.: Basic Books, 1969.

69. Hofsten, Erland, cited in a news item, *N.Y. Post,* June 14, 1972.

70. "Homosexuality in the Male: Report of the Findings and Conclusions of an Eleven-Member Psychiatric Study Group." *Int. J. of Psychiatry.* Vol. 11, no. 4, 1973.

71. Huxley, Aldous. *Point Counterpoint.* N.Y.: Literary Guild, 1928.

72. Huxley, Julian. *Evolution, the Modern Synthesis.* N.Y.: 1942.

73. Jacobson, E. *The Self and the Object World.* N.Y.: International Universities Press, 1964.

74. Johnson, Virginia E., and Masters, William H. *Human Sexual Response.* Boston: Little, Brown, 1966.

75. Johnson, Virginia E., Masters, William H. *Human Sexual Inadequacy.* Boston: Little, Brown, 1970.

76. Jones, Ernest. "Early Development of Female Homosexuality." *Int. J. Psychoanal.* 8:459–472, 1927.

77. Kahn, Herman, quoted in "The Mind: From Memory Pills to Electronic Pleasures Beyond Sex." *Time.* April 19, 1971, p. 47.

78. Kahn, Herman, and Bruce-Briggs, B. *Things to Come.* N.Y.: Macmillan, 1972.

79. Kallman, F. J. "Comparative Twin Studies of the Genetic Aspects of Male Homosexuality." *J. Nerv. & Mental Diseases,* 115:283–298, 1952.

80. Kaplan, Helen S. "Psychosis Associated with Marijuana." *N.Y. State Journal of Medicine.* Feb. 15, 1971, pp. 433–435.

81. Kardiner, A. *The Individual and His Society: The Psychodynamics of Primitive Social Organizations.* N.Y.: Columbia, 1939.

82. Kardiner, A. *The Psychological Frontiers of Society.* N.Y.: Columbia, 1945.

83. Kardiner, A. *Sex and Morality.* N.Y.: Bobbs-Merrill, 1954.

84. Kardiner, A. Personal communication to the author, 1973.

85. Karlen, Arno. *Sexuality and Homosexuality.* N.Y.: Norton, 1971.

86. Kass, Leon. Quoted in "Grave New World." *Saturday Review.* April 8, 1972. pp. 26–27.

87. Kinsey, A. C., Pomeroy, W. B., and Martin, C. E. *Sexual Behavior in the Human Male.* Philadelphia: W. B. Saunders, 1948.

88. Kinsey, A. C., Pomeroy, W. B., Martin, C. E., and Gebhard,

P. H. *Sexual Behavior in the Human Female.* Philadelphia: W. B. Saunders, 1953.

89. Klein, Melanie. *The Psychoanalysis of Children.* London: Hogarth Press, 1954.

90. Klein, Melanie. *Our Adult World.* N.Y.: Basic Books, 1963.

91. Koestler, Arthur. *The Ghost and the Machine.* N.Y.: Macmillan, 1967.

92. Kronhausen, Phyllis C. and Ebehard W. "The Psychology of Pornography" in *The Encyclopedia of Sexual Behavior,* edited by Ellis, A., and Abarbanel, A. N.Y.: Hawthorn Books, 1961.

93. Kutschisky, Berl. Quoted in a news item, *N.Y. Times,* Nov. 9, 1970.

94. Lacey F. K. *The Family in Classical Greece.* Ithaca, N.Y.: Cornell, 1968.

95. Lawrence, D. H. "Pornography and Obscenity: An Essay." N.Y.: Knopf, 1930, pp. 1–40.

96. Lerner, Gerda. "The Feminist: A Second Look." *Columbia Forum.* 13:24–30, 1972.

97. Levy, David M. "Maternal Feelings Toward the Newborn," in *World Federation for Mental Health: Mental Health in Home and School.* London: H. K. Lewis, 1958.

98. Lichtenstein, H. "Identity and Sexuality." *J. of the Amer. Psychoanal. Assoc.* Vol. 9, 1961, pp. 179–260.

99. Lichtenstein, H. "The Psychoanalytic Psychotherapy in a World in Crisis." *Int. J. of Psychoanalytic Psychotherapy.* Vol. 2, no. 2, 1973, pp. 149–173.

100. Lifton, Robert J. *Thought Reform and the Psychology of Totalism.* N.Y.: Norton, 1961.

101. Lorand, Sandor. "The Therapy of Perversions," in *Perversions: Psychodynamics and Therapy.* ed. Lorand, S., and Balint, M. N.Y.: Random House, 1956, pp. 290–307.

102. Lorenz, Konrad. *On Aggression.* N.Y.: Harcourt, Brace & World, 1963.

103. Mahler, M. S., and Gosliner, B. J. "On Symbiotic Child Psychosis: Genetic, Dynamic and Restitutive Aspects." *Psychoanalytic Study of the Child.* 10:195–211. N.Y.: International Universities Press, 1955.

104. Mahler, M. S. *On Human Symbiosis and the Vicissitudes of*

*Individuation* N.Y.: International Universities Press, 1968.

105. Margolis, Herbert, and Rubenstein, Paul. *The Group Sex Tapes.* N.Y.: Paperback Library, 1971.

106. "Marijuana and Health: A Report to Congress." *Amer. J. Psychiatry.* Vol. 128, Part 2, Aug. 1971.

107. Marmor, J., editor. *Sexual Inversion.* N.Y.: Basic Books, 1965.

108. Mass. General Hospital. "Research in Genetics: For Good or Evil?" *Mass. General Hosp. News.* 30:5, May 1971, pp. 7–8.

109. Mead, Margaret. *Sex and Temperament in Three Primitive Societies.* N.Y.: Morrow, 1963.

110. Mead, Margaret. "Life Cycle and Its Variations: the Division of Roads." *Daedalus: The Journal of the American Academy of Arts and Sciences.* Summer. Vol. 1967 entitled "Toward the Year 2000: Work in Progress."

111. Mead, Margaret. *Culture and Commitment.* N.Y.: Doubleday, 1970.

112. Meierhofer, Marie. In "Depression in 3-Month Old Infants." *Medical Tribune.* Vol. 13, no. 14, March 5, 1972.

113. Millett, Kate. *Sexual Politics.* N.Y.: Doubleday, 1970.

114. Money, John. "Pornography in the Home: A Topic in Medical Education," in *Contemporary Sexual Behavior: Critical Issues in the 1970's.* Zubin, Joseph, and Money, John. eds. Baltimore: Johns Hopkins, 1973.

115. Morris, Desmond. *The Naked Ape.* N.Y.: McGraw-Hill, 1967.

116. Mumford, Lewis. *In the Name of Sanity.* N.Y.: Harcourt, Brace, 1954.

117. Mumford, Lewis. *The Myth of the Machine: The Pentagon of Power.* N.Y.: Harcourt, Brace, Jovanovich, 1964.

118. Mumford, Lewis. Quoted in *Newsweek.* July 7, 1969, p. 61.

119. National Institutes of Mental Health. Washington D.C. Report of the Task Force on Homosexuality. Oct. 10, 1969.

120. Nemy, Enid. *N.Y. Times.* Oct. 2, 1972.

121. Olds, James. *Scientific American.* 1956, p. 195.

122. Oraison, M. *Illusions and Anxiety.* N.Y.: Macmillan, 1953.

123. Orwell, George. *1984.* N.Y.: Harcourt, Brace, 1949.

124. Rado, Sandor. "An Adaptational View of Sexual Behavior," in *Psychosexual Development in Health and Disease.* Hoch, P., and Zubin, J., eds. N.Y.: Grune and Stratton, 1949, pp. 159–189.

125. Rado, Sandor. "Narcotic Bondage: A General Theory of the Dependence on Narcotic Drugs" (1957), in *The Collected Papers of Sandor Rado,* vol. II, N.Y.: Grune & Stratton, 1962, pp. 21–29.

126. Rado, Sandor. *Psychoanalysis of Behavior: The Collected Papers of Sandor Rado,* vols. I & II. N.Y.: Grune & Stratton, 1962.

127. Ricoeur, P. *Freud and Philosophy: An Essay on Interpretation.* New Haven: Yale, 1970.

128. Rieff, Philip. *Freud: The Mind of the Moralist.* N.Y.: Viking, 1959.

129. Rivers, Caryl. "Grave New World." *Saturday Review.* April 8, 1972, pp. 23–27.

130. Romm, May E. "Effects of the Mother-Child Relationship and the Father-Child Relationship on Psychosexual Development." *Medical Aspects of Human Sexuality.* Vol. 3, no. 2, Feb. 1969.

131. Rorvik, David M. "The Test Tube Baby Is Coming." *Look.* May 18, 1971, pp. 83–88.

132. Rosen, Ismond, editor. *The Pathology and Treatment of Sexual Deviation.* London: Oxford, 1964.

133. Rosenfeld, Albert. "Procreation Without Sex." *Physicians' World.* May, 1973, pp. 61–63.

134. Roszak, Betty and Theodore. *Masculine/Feminine.* N.Y.: Harper Colophon, 1969.

135. Ruitenbeek, Hendrik, M., editor. *The Problem of Homosexuality in Modern Society.* N.Y.: Dutton, 1963.

136. Sachs, Hans. "On the Genesis of Sexual Perversions." *Int. Z. Psychoanal.,* 172–182, 1929 (Tr. Hella Freud Bernays, 1964; N.Y. Psychoanalytic Institute Library.)

137. Sagarin, Edward. *Odd Man In: Societies of Deviants in America.* Chicago: Quadrangle, 1969.

138. Saussure, R. de. "Homosexual Fixations in Neurotic Women." *Rev. Franc. Psychanal.* 3:50–91, 1929. (Tr. Hella Freud Bernays, 1961; N.Y. Psychoanalytic Institute Library.)

139. Scarf, Maggie. "He and She: The Sex Hormones and Behavior." *N.Y. Times Magazine.* May 7, 1972.

140. Schmeck, Harold M. "Two Doctors Urge a Halt in Human Genetics Engineering." *N.Y. Times.* March 9, 1972.

141. Sherrington, Sir Charles. *The Brain and Its Mechanism.* Cambridge University Press, 1933.

142. Sinsheimer, Robert, quoted in "Man Into Superman: The Promise and Peril of the New Genetics." *Time.* April 19, 1971, pp. 35–51.

143. Skinner, B. F. *Beyond Freedom and Dignity.* N.Y.: Knopf, 1971.

144. Socarides, C. W. "Meaning and Content of a Pedophiliac Perversion." *J. of the Amer. Psychoanal. Assn.* 7:84–94, 1959.

145. Socarides, C. W. "The Development of a Fetishistic Perversion." *J. of the Amer. Psychoanal. Assn.* 8:281–311, 1960.

146. Socarides, C. W. "Theoretical and Clinical Aspects of Overt Male Homosexuality." *J. of the Amer. Psychoanal. Assn.* 8:552–566, 1960.

147. Socarides, C. W. "Theoretical and Clinical Aspects of Overt Female Homosexuality." *J. of the Amer. Psychoanal. Assn.* 10:579–502, 1962.

148. Socarides, C. W. "The Historical Development of Theoretical and Clinical Aspects of Female Homosexuality." *J. of the Amer. Psychoanal. Assn.* 11:386–414, 1963.

149. Socarides, C. W. "Female Homosexuality," in *Sexual Behavior and the Law,* Slovenko, R. ed. Springfield, Ill.: Chas. C. Thomas, 1965.

150. Socarides, C. W. "On Vengeance: The Desire to 'Get Even.'" *J. of the Amer. Psychoanal. Assn.* 14:356–375, 1966.

151. Socarides, C. W. "A Provisional Theory of Aetiology in Male Homosexuality: A Case of Pre-oedipal Origin." *Int. J. Psycho-Anal.* 49:27–37, 1968.

152. Socarides, C. W. *The Overt Homosexual.* N.Y.: Grune & Stratton 1968. Curtis Publishing Co., 1970. Reissued by Jason Aronson, N.Y., 1974 (*L'Homosexualité.* Paris: Payot. *Der Offen Homosexuelle.* Surkamp Verlag).

153. Socarides, C. W. "Desarrollo Historico do los Conceptos Teoricos y Clinicos Sobre Homosexualidad Femenina Evidente," in *La Homosexualidad Femenina,* R. Alsonso, editor. Buenos Aires: Talleres Graficos Lumen, 1969.

154. Socarides, C. W. "The Desire for Sexual Transformation: A Psychiatric Evaluation of 'Transsexualism.'" *Am. J. Psychiatry.* 125:1419–1425, 1969.

155. Socarides, C. W. "The Psychoanalytic Therapy of a Male Homosexual." *Psychoanal. Quart.* 38:173–190, 1969.

156. Socarides, C. W. "A Psychoanalytic Study of the Desire for Sexual Transformation (Transsexualism): The Plaster-of-Paris Man." *Int. J. of Psychoanal.* 51:341–349, 1970.

157. Socarides, C. W. "Homosexuality and Medicine." *Journal of the A.M.A.* vol. 212, May 18, 1970.

158. Socarides, C. W. "Pornography and Obscenity." Report before the sub-committee on Postal Operations, U.S. House of Representatives, Nov. 1970.

159. Socarides, C. W. "Homosexuality—Basic Concepts and Psychodynamics." *Int. J. of Psychiat.* 10:118–125, 1972.

160. Socarides, C. W. "Sexual Perversion and the Fear of Engulfment." *Int. J. of Psychoanalytic Psychotherapy.* vol. 2, no. 4, Nov., 1973.

161. Socarides, C. W. "The Demonified Mother: A Study of Voyeurism and Sexual Sadism." *Int. J. of Psychoanal.* vol. 1, no. 2, 1974.

162. Socarides, C. W. "Homosexuality," in *The American Handbook of Psychiatry,* second edition. N.Y.: Basic Books. 1974.

163. Spitz, R. *The First Year of Life: A Psychoanalytic Study of Normal and Deviant Development of Object Relations.* N.Y.: International Universities Press, 1965.

164. Spitz, R. *A Genetic Field Theory of Ego Formation.* N.Y.: International Universities Press, 1959.

165. Stoller, Robert. *Sex and Gender.* N.Y.: Science House, 1968.

166. Stoller, Robert. Personal communication. May 14, 1969.

167. "Sweden Today: The Status of Women in Sweden." Report to the United Nations, 1968. Article in brochure form. Swedish Institute, Box 3306, Stockholm 3 Sweden.

168. Symmers, W. St. C. "Carcinoma of the Breast in Transsexual Individuals After Surgical and Hormonal Inter-

ference with the Primary and Secondary Sex Characteristics." *British Medical Journal*. Vol. 2, 1968, pp. 83–85.

169. Szent-Gyorgyi, Albert. *The Crazy Ape*. N.Y.: Philosophical Library, 1970.

170. Taylor, John, quoted in "The Mind: From Memory Pills to Electronic Pleasures Beyond Sex." *Time*. April 19, 1971, p. 47.

171. Teal, Don. *The Gay Militants*. N.Y.: Stein & Day, 1971.

172. "The Problem of Homosexuality." N.Y. Academy of Medicine. *Bulletin*. 40:576–580, 1964.

173. *The Report of the Commission on Obscenity and Pornography*. N.Y.: Bantam, 1970.

174. Thompson, W. I. *At the Edge of History: Speculations on the Transformation of Culture*. N.Y.: Harper & Row, 1971.

175. Toffler, Alvin. *Future Shock*. N.Y.: Random House, 1970.

176. Trilling, Lionel. *Freud and the Crisis of Our Culture*. Boston: Beacon, 1955.

177. Van der Leeuw, P. J. "The Preoedipal Phase of the Male." *Psychoanal. Study of the Child*. Vol. 13, 1958.

178. Wald, George, quoted in "Grave New World." *Saturday Review*. April 8, 1972, p. 27.

179. Watson, James D. "Moving Toward Clonal Man." *Atlantic Monthly*. 1971, pp. 50–53.

180. Weiss, Eduardo. *The Structure and Dynamics of the Human Mind*. N.Y.: Grune & Stratton, 1960.

181. West, L. J. *Modern Medicine*. Dec. 16, 1968.

182. Williams, Tennessee. *Confessional*. Produced in N.Y. under the title *Small Craft Warnings*. N.Y.: New Directions, 1970.

183. Wolfenden, J. *Report of the Committee on Homosexual Offences and Prostitution*. London: H. M. Stationery Office (Cmnd 247), 1967.

184. Woodger, J. H. *Levels of Integration in Biological and Social Systems*. University of Chicago Press, 1942.

185. Wylie, Philip. *A Generation of Vipers*. N.Y.: Rinehart & Co., 1942.

186. Zilboorg, Gregory. *History of Medical Psychology*. N.Y.: Norton, 1941.

187. Zweig, Stefan. *Mental Healers*. London: Caselle Press, 1933.

# INDEX